Kid Tips for Walt Disney World

Touring Advice by Kids for Kids

Tracie A. Cook

Published by Vacation Field Guides
P.O. Box 366, Pleasant Lake, MI 49272
http://vacationfieldguides.com

ISBN: 978-0-615-35656-3
Edition: 1.1

Printed in the United States of America

Every effort has been made to ensure the accuracy of information in this book; however, the publisher and author assume no responsibility for errors or omissions. Attractions and schedules are constantly changing. Since most of the material is reader opinion, the author and publisher cannot be held responsible for the experiences of readers while traveling.

Dedication

To my mom, Marsha.
Thank you for introducing me
to the Magic and for always encouraging me to
follow my dreams.

Many Thanks

I could not have created this book without the many people who helped along the way. I owe a huge thank you to the Disney Internet community: Pete Werner and Corey Martin from wdwinfo.com, for allowing me to post that I was looking for Kid Tips; Ricky Brigante from insidethemagic.net, for announcing that I was writing this book and seeking tips; and Robin Frohm from themagicforless.com, for taking my cover design and converting it into the correct format. This book was made possible because of their support.

Additionally, I wish to thank my family for their encouragement: my husband, Paul, whose insight and comments helped me turn this dream into a reality; Alden and William, the young men in our family, for letting me see the wonder of the parks through their eyes over the many trips we have taken as a family; Brent and Angela, my brother and sister, thank you for sharing in my love of Walt Disney World, as only siblings can.

Many thanks also go to Diane Long for her technical support, Shannon Clark for her valued opinion, and Kendra Magnus for being a true friend and amazing editor.

Finally, I owe a very special thank you to all the kids who took the time to share their advice. I have enjoyed reading each and every one of your tips, and I am excited to give your opinions a voice.

Contents

A Magical Vacation

Whether your family is planning a trip to Walt Disney World, have already been, or is hoping to visit soon, *Kid Tips for Walt Disney World* is full of information to help you make the most of your trip. With four theme parks, two water parks, and dozens of restaurants, Walt Disney World is a big place. It can be hard to decide where to start and what to do next.

All the tips in this book are written by kids, *just like you.* You'll learn the rides that kids rate as awesome (worth waiting in line for twice) and which ones might be ok to skip (come back when there are no lines). You'll find out where the best places are to get your favorite character's autograph and see what restaurants kids *really* like. Discover what fun you can have at the water parks, Downtown Disney, and your Disney resort.

In the back of this book, there's a spot for you to keep track of your must-see attractions and to write your own tips. You'll also find packing suggestions from other Kid Tipsters and a "Lost Card" to slip into your pocket.

No matter what you decide to do on your trip, I know that your whole family is going to have a great time!

Have a Magical Trip!
Tracie A. Cook

Meet the Kid Tipsters

Kid Tipsters from across the United States, Canada, Europe, and Mexico shared their tips about visiting Walt Disney World. So, what is a tip? A tip is really just a piece of advice. You don't have to follow all of the tips in this book, but you'll have a good idea what other kids found helpful.

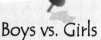

Boys vs. Girls

The number of boys and girls who contributed to this book is almost equal.

Boys: 48%
Girls: 52%

Ages

Kid Tipsters are between the ages of 7 and 15 years old.

Tips Received

More than **8000 tips** were submitted!

100% of Kid Tipsters said that they would like to go back to Walt Disney World again.

Walt Disney World Today

MAGIC KINGDOM

EPCOT

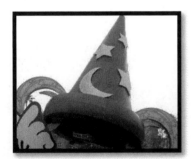

DISNEY'S HOLLYWOOD STUDIOS

DISNEY'S ANIMAL KINGDOM

Disney Speak

Some of the words you might read in this book or hear around Walt Disney World were created by Walt Disney and his Imagineers. Look over the list and before you know it, you'll be talking like a Kid Tipster in no time!

Attraction: Any theme park ride or show.

Audio-Animatronic: Life-like animals and humans that seem real but are really robots.

Cast Member: A Disney employee.

Extra Magic Hours: Additional hours in which only Disney resort guests can be in the parks and ride the attractions. Check a park's Times Guide for more information.

Fastpass: A special attraction pass you can get so you don't have to wait in line for the most popular attractions. Look at a park guide map to see which attractions have Fastpass available.

Guest: A visitor to Walt Disney World.

Guide Map: A theme park map that describes the attractions, shops, and restaurants.

Hidden Mickey: Three circles that form the head and two ears of Mickey Mouse. Imagineers hide them all over the parks, hotels, and restaurants.

Imagineers: The creative people who start with an idea and bring it to life in the parks.

Pavilion: Buildings at Epcot that house the attractions.

Preshow: The entertainment leading up to the main attraction or show.

Queue: The line you wait in before you get to see a show or board an attraction.

Stand-by line: If an attraction has Fastpass available, there are two lines. One line is for guests with a Fastpass. The other line, or stand-by-line, is for guests without a Fastpass.

Times Guide: A piece of paper that lists when shows start, how late the park is open, and what times characters can be seen.

Know Before You Go

Planning a trip to Walt Disney World is lots of fun. But before you get your suitcase out, read through these practical tips to help your vacation go smoothly.

Plan beforehand. There is a lot to see at Walt Disney World, and you can't do everything in one trip. Figure out what you want to see or do before you go.

Eric, age 11, Lockport, IL

William planning his day

Try something new. Just because you think you might not like something, try it anyway. It might be a ride or show or food. You never know, you might like it.

Alex, age 9, Gardner, KS

Crowds will happen. Depending on when you come for a visit, there may be crowds and you will have to wait in line. Instead of getting grumpy, make a game out of it—play I spy—many queue areas have lots of neat things to look at and listen to.

Savannah, age 8, Clermont, FL

Get to the parks early. Even though it is a vacation, get up early so you can be at the park opening. It is a lot less crowded then, and you can ride and see a lot more things.

Morgan, age 14, Atlanta, GA

Save time in line. Don't forget to use Fastpass tickets. They help you save time on the most popular rides.

Chloe, age 9, Okemos, MI

Take a closer look. I think everyone should slow down a bit and enjoy the theming in all of the parks. Disney pays so much attention to detail that even the garbage cans match the land or area they are in.

Sam, age 11, Schaumburg, IL

Search for Hidden Mickeys. There are lots of cool Hidden Mickeys everywhere. They are fun to try to find. We look for them when we get bored waiting in line. You can buy a Hidden Mickey book that will help you find where they are all located.

Alexis, age 13, Washington, NJ

Cast Members can help you. If you get lost, find a person that works there—they have the special name tags. They'll help you find your parents.

Jake, age 9, Denver, PA

Stay Safe. Follow all the safety rules and directions from Cast Members.

Emily, age 13, Houston, TX

Help in each park. If you get bitten or hurt, go to one of the First Aid stations for help. They are very helpful. You can find them in every park.

Jeremy, age 11, Seattle, WA

Stay hydrated. Drink plenty of water! I like to bring my own water bottle and fill it up at the drinking fountains. Disney sells a strap that will fit over your water bottle so you can easily carry it around the park.

George, age 11, Newark, CA

Beat the heat. If you are going in a hot season, it is good to bring power misters so you don't get too hot. They also sell them in the parks.

Sara, age 9, Rochester, NY

Prepare for the cold. If you are going to Disney World in the winter months, make sure you bring a sweatshirt. It can get chilly, even in Florida.

Matt, age 11, West Chester, PA

Rain, Rain, Rain. Florida gets a lot of rain, especially in the summer. Remind your parents to bring rain ponchos. Mine were always left in the room.

Caleb, age 8, Houston, TX

Sun protection is a must! Make sure you wear sunglasses and plenty of sunscreen!

Madelynne, age 9, Charleston, MO

Your shoes are important. Wear comfy shoes and be ready to walk a lot!

Daniel, age 10, Severn, MD

Eat with the characters. Character meals are the best places to see the characters. We like to have sit-down dinners to rest from the rides. Characters make it like you are still at the parks! I got tons of autographs!

Jonathan, age 9, Canonsburg, PA

Have an autograph book. Bring a pen or pencil and an autograph book because you never know who you are going to meet. I have even met Captain Hook when we were just walking to the nearest bathroom!

Collin, age 8, Pearl River, NY

Pack with success. Make a packing list and check off everything when you put it in your bag. Bring the list so you can do the same thing before you come home so you don't forget anything.

Jillian, age 15, Ottawa, Canada

A small light can come in handy. Some of the rides at Disney are in the dark. Bring a little flashlight to wear around your neck if you are afraid.

Kent, age 7, Las Vegas, NV

Capture the moment. Make sure you bring a camera to Disney World so you can capture your own special memories!

Alexis, age 14, Wesley Chapel, FL

Picture-perfect pictures. The parks have photographers all throughout them so that they can take your picture and put the picture on your Photopass card. Sometimes, the photographers

will digitally put in characters or borders to add the Disney touch. At the end of your trip, you can review your pictures online and pick out the ones you want to buy.

Madlyn, age 13, Bardstown, KY

Try pin trading. Buy some Disney pins and find a cast member wearing a lanyard. If you see a pin that you want, you can ask to trade one of your pins for the pin that you want. It is a fun way to interact with the people who work at Disney, and it lets you "shop" without spending a lot of money. We display ours on a corkboard for everyone to admire.

Hunter, age 11, Woodland Park, CO

Press a penny or quarter. There are machines all over WDW where you can press a design into a penny. You can even buy a book to put all of your pennies in. The penny machines cost two quarters and a penny. My mom puts all our pennies and quarters in a tube so that they are ready when we get to Disney.

Carrie, age 8, Columbus, OH

Have extra fun for free. I love to do the Kim Possible missions at Epcot and the Discovery stations at Animal Kingdom. You learn a lot and the best part is that it doesn't cost anything.

Belle, age 9, Atlanta, GA

Different ways to travel. The monorails are really cool and a fun way to get around some of the Disney Parks. There are also boats you can take places, and of course, there are a ton of buses. Use the time you spend getting to the parks to plan your day.

Joseph, age 11, Albany, NY

Find time for homework. Get your homework done in your spare time. Try and get as much done before or on the way there as you can and do some during resting time. Don't leave it all for the end of the trip, and be willing to make up anything you have missed.

Kyle, age 11, Bristol, VA

Be on your best behavior. Listen to your parents because you don't want to be punished on vacation.

Michael, age 8, South Hackensack, NJ

Every day is a day to celebrate. You can celebrate your birthday there or any other special occasion. Each park has free buttons at guest services.

Seth, age 11, Florence, AL

Have fun! Enjoy the time you are there. It is so much fun and it goes by fast!

Marian, age 12, Loudonville, NY

Magic Kingdom

Fun for all ages. The Magic Kingdom is broken up into themed lands. I love all the rides at the Magic Kingdom because they can be enjoyed by my entire family!

Delainey, age 8, Tinley Park, IL

Be there at opening. Try to see the park opening ceremony. The characters come out, they play music, and it's a great way to start your day at the Magic Kingdom.

Cameron, age 10, Palmyra, PA

Parades and shows not to be missed. Be sure to check the times for the parades and shows. Magic Kingdom shows are always so much fun to watch! And you have to be sure to catch the Wishes fireworks show at least one night that you're there!

Ashley, age 9, Philadelphia, PA

Fastpass popular attractions. Make sure you get Fastpasses to either Buzz Lightyear or any of the three mountains shortly after you enter the park because those are great attractions, and they usually get very long lines in the afternoon.

Andy, age 13, Crystal Lakes, IL

Kids' Vote

Kid Tipsters rated all of the attractions at Walt Disney World. Look for the Kid Tip Top Pick flag throughout the book. You'll find it beside the best of the best Disney attractions.

Favorite Park

Kid Tipsters voted the Magic Kingdom as their favorite park.

Best Land

Tomorrowland is where most of our readers like to spend their time.

Best Fireworks

Wishes was voted the best nighttime fireworks show.

The Magic Kingdom is home to 7 Kid Tip Top Pick attractions.

Attraction Ratings

OK

- Swiss Family Treehouse
- Tom Sawyer Island
- Country Bear Jamboree
- Frontierland Shootin' Arcade
- The Hall of Presidents
- Stitch's Great Escape!
- Railroad

Good

- The Enchanted Tiki Room
- The Magic Carpets of Aladdin
- Jungle Cruise
- Liberty Square Riverboat
- Prince Charming Regal Carrousel
- Dumbo
- Snow White's Scary Adventures
- Winnie the Pooh
- Astro Orbiter
- Carousel of Progress

Awesome

- Pirates of the Caribbean
- Splash Mountain
- Big Thunder Mountain Railroad
- Haunted Mansion
- It's a Small World
- Peter Pan's Flight
- Mickey's PhilharMagic
- Mad Tea Party
- Tomorrowland Speedway
- Space Mountain
- Tomorrowland Transit Author
- Buzz Lightyear's Space Ranger Spin
- Monsters, Inc. Laugh Floor

Attraction Tips

SWISS FAMILY TREEHOUSE

Climb high above Adventureland. I really like all the different rooms in the tree house and getting to see how the Robinsons lived. This attraction usually doesn't have a line, so see it after you have gone on the bigger attractions.

Hayden, age 12, New Madrid, MO

THE MAGIC CARPETS OF ALADDIN

Soar over Agrabah. This ride is a lot like Dumbo. You sit in a huge flying carpet. If you're in the front seat, you get to control how high or low your flying carpet flies.

Carter, age 8, Morgan City, LA

Dodge wild camels. I really like the spitting camels. They spit water as you go by them.

Isabella, age 8, Newark, NJ

THE ENCHANTED TIKI ROOM

All the birds sing words. Iago and Zazu have taken over the Tiki Room. There is lots of singing and dancing birds. This show is full of surprises, including a very funny Iago!

Carissa, age 8, Savage, MN

PIRATES OF THE CARIBBEAN Kid Tip
Top Pick

Dodge shooting cannons. You ride a boat through a town that's just been attacked by cursed pirates. There's a part where you go past their ship and they are shooting cannons and it seems so real. I like the music that plays throughout the ride, and I like to see all the different scenes. It's awesome!

Jared, age 14, Tacoma, WA

See Captain Jack Sparrow. If you go to Disney World and don't ride Pirates of the Caribbean you will regret it, believe me. Captain Jack Sparrow looks just like the one in the movie. At the beginning you go through some mist that has Davy Jones's face on it, then you go down a small drop! This ride is great!

Stephanie, age 8, Ontario, Canada

Shop for treasure. My favorite gift shop is at the end of Pirates of the Caribbean. You can buy all kinds of pirate stuff.

Jared, age 10, Savannah, GA

JUNGLE CRUISE

Travel through the jungle. You sit in a boat and travel outside though the jungle. Unlike Animal Kingdom, the animals here are all fake. The guides tell very corny jokes. My favorite part is when it looks like the elephants are going to spray you, but you don't get wet. This ride is fun for the whole family!

Daniel, age 10, Ontario, Canada

SPLASH MOUNTAIN
Kid Tip
Top Pick

Two rides in one. I like Splash Mountain the best because it's two rides in one.  I like the scenes with the singing animals you see as you travel along the water. I like the surprise drops, and I like the grand finale with the log shooting down the mountain. It really cools you off on a hot day.

Alison, age 10, Pasadena, CA

You may get wet or soaked. Make sure to sit in the front seat because you get really wet and you can see Frontierland very well. One time we rode when the fireworks were going off. It was an awesome view.

Isaiah, age 8, Dothan, AL

Before you drop, say "cheese." Splash Mountain is a longer ride than others so it's worth the wait, and a good way to cool off. We always get a family picture. The camera is right as you drop, so we always pretend like we are scared or look silly.

Ryan, age 9, Emerson, NJ

BIG THUNDER MOUNTAIN RAILROAD
Kid Tip
Top Pick

Good for first timers. Big Thunder Mountain Railroad is a good roller coaster for beginners because it does not go upside down and it's outside so you can see where you're going.

Brian, age 9, Bibbsboro, NJ

Board a runaway train. It really feels like you are on a runaway train through the desert mountains. My favorite part of the ride is when you go through the mine and all of these rocks are falling at you, and then you all of a sudden go down a drop!

Natalie, age 13, Manchester, England

The back is wilder. When you ride in the back of the train everything is bumpier and faster which makes for a great roller coaster. Riding at night in the dark is even better!

Rocco, age 12, Pennsauken, NJ

Tom Sawyer Island

Explore mysterious caves. Tom Sawyer Island is really fun! There is a dock in Frontierland where you take a raft to the island. There are lots of cool things to do while you are there. There is a playground, an Indian town, a fort, and other fun stuff.

Michael, age 10, Columbus, OH

Search for a surprise. If you go to the island early in the morning, you might find a paintbrush. If you find one, you can give it to the Cast Member at the rafts, and they will give you a free Fastpass. I really enjoy looking for the paintbrushes!

Elizabeth, age 13,
Seymour, WI

THE HAUNTED MANSION

A scare-tacular good time. I think younger kids might find this ride a little scary. But it's a lot of fun! You start in a stretching room, and then you move though the mansion to your awaiting Doombuggy. A ghost will even hitchhike in your Doombuggy at the end!!

Carter, age 10, San Francisco, CA

Funny, spooky tombstones. Make sure you read the tombstones when you walk in the mansion. They have hilarious epitaphs on them, for example: "Here lies good old Fred. A great big rock fell on his head."

Ashton, age 13, Rochester, NY

Hidden Mickey alert. My favorite part is the ballroom. All the ghosts are dancing and there is a hidden Mickey on the table made up of plates.

Cora, age 8, Waterbury, CT

LIBERTY SQUARE RIVERBOAT

Live like an adventurer. The riverboat travels around Tom Sawyer Island. There are different rooms to see on the boat and you'll hear about Mark Twain and life on the Mississippi. I like all the cool scenes you pass around the river.

John, age 11, Franklin, TN

THE HALL OF PRESIDENTS

See our past leaders up close. Wow! The presidents look so real! You enter the theater and see a short history movie. Then the curtain opens and all of our past presidents are on stage. It's neat to see the stuff you've learned in history come to life.

Madison, age 13, Louisville, KY

Celebrate being an American. Everyone should see this attraction at least once. It's good to learn about our country and see how far we have come. You can also take a break and cool off.

Wyatt, age 10, Pasadena, CA

"IT'S A SMALL WORLD"

For the young and young at heart. I like "It's a Small World" because it is very cute and cool and my whole family can go on it together no matter how old or young we are.

Alana, age 7,
Rochester, NY

Sing along! The cute dolls sing the same song in their own country's language. By the end of the boat ride, you'll be singing the song, too!

Claire, age 10, Fenton, MO

PETER PAN'S FLIGHT

Fly to Never Land. Peter Pan's Flight is my favorite ride in Fantasyland. It's really neat how the ship really flies through the air and the cars look so real when you fly over London. You will need to use a Fastpass or expect to wait in a very long line.

Jacob, age 12, Pittsburgh, PA

Classic Disney attraction. I never get tired of going on Peter Pan. I love how it feels like you are flying. Everyone should go on this ride at least once. If you want to go again, I would definitely get a Fastpass! The lines are always long for Peter Pan and there is not a lot to see when you are waiting in line.

Angie, age 11, Elkhart, IL

MICKEY'S PHILHARMAGIC
Kid Tip
Top Pick

3-D musical misadventure. Mickey's PhilharMagic is a fun tour through classic Disney movies. Donald Duck is really funny. The 3-D and special effects are amazing. Plus, it's a great air conditioned theater, so you get out of the Florida heat for a while.

Andrew, age 10, Penfield, NY

Every seat is a good one. Even though PhilharMagic is not a ride, it's my favorite attraction because it feels like you're on a ride when you watch the show. The characters look like they are right in front of only you.

Cass, age 8, Springfield, IL

SNOW WHITE'S SCARY ADVENTURE

Ride through the spooky Enchanted Forest. This ride is not

for kids who get scared easily. The wicked witch is scary looking. I like the end when you see the dwarfs waving goodbye to you.

Taylor, age 13,
Clemson, SC

They all lived happily ever after. Snow White usually doesn't have a long line, so you can save it for the end. My younger sister was a little scared, but not as scared as when she rode the Haunted Mansion. The ride has a happy ending.

Lauren, age 12, Kalamazoo, MI

DUMBO THE FLYING ELEPHANT

Magical at all ages. When you go to the Magic Kingdom, make sure that Dumbo is the first ride you ride at opening time. Otherwise it is a long line. As old as you are, it is still fun and special.

Brendan, age 10, Imperial, MO

Soar through the fireworks. Tell your parents you want to ride Dumbo during the fireworks. It's way better than watching them from the ground.

Heather, age 8, Collierville, TN

PRINCE CHARMING REGAL CARROUSEL

A horse fit for a princess. Be sure to ride Cinderella's horse on the carousel. It's the one with the purple flowers on its neck and gold ribbon around its tail.

Jenna, age 8, Sumrall, MS

THE MANY ADVENTURES OF WINNIE THE POOH

Jump into a book. You sit in a giant honey pot. I think it's awesome being in the whole Hundred Acre Woods story. All the characters are there. When you're leaving, listen for Tigger to say "Ta-ta for now!"

Alanna, age 11, London, Canada

TOMORROWLAND SPEEDWAY

No driver's license needed. I like the Speedway because usually kids my age can't drive real cars, but you get to here and it is really fun!

Katie, age 10, Puyallup, WA

Drive your parents around. I have so much fun trying to stay on the course, but I never do. I have fun bouncing my Mom around. If you are tall enough, you can drive alone in the car and your parents can watch you circle the track.

T.J., age 9, Mobile, AL

SPACE MOUNTAIN

**Kid Tip
Top Pick**

Rocket into space. This rollercoaster only has a few drops that aren't too steep. When you are on Space Mountain, the room you are in is completely dark except there are stars and planets all around you, so it actually feels like you are on a rocket in space!

Matthew, age 9, Littleton, CO

Total darkness. Being in the dark makes this rollercoaster way more fun. The drops and turns are the best because you don't know where you're going next.

Christopher, age 12, Robertsdale, AL

Rest in the arcade. There is an arcade at the end of this ride. If you're too scared to ride, or you have younger brothers and sisters, they can wait in there and play some games and cool off.

Samantha, age 11, Fishersville, KY

ASTRO ORBITER

Soar among the planets. This ride is similar to Dumbo but way cooler! You fly really high up in the air. I could see the hotels outside the park. I wouldn't recommend this ride if you are afraid of heights.

Kyle, age 11, Joppa, MD

TOMORROWLAND TRANSIT AUTHORITY

A highway in the sky. If you go on the Tomorrowland Transit Authority before riding any other rides in Tomorrowland, you get to see an overview of most of the rides before tackling them!

Chris, age 12, Syracuse, NY

Launch to the hoverburbs. Listen to the story as you ride along. It sounds like you are visiting another planet. There are some parts that are in total darkness, just so you know.

Adrian, age 9, Highlands Ranch, CO

WALT DISNEY'S CAROUSEL OF PROGRESS

Family, friendly fun. The Carousel of Progress is a family friendly ride. I recommend kids and tweens see it at least once. Instead of the stage moving, you actually move around the stage. Look for a hidden Mickey Mouse doll in the last scene.

Colleen, age 10, Springfield, IL

A Disney original. I enjoy seeing all the different time periods and listening to the song. I also like knowing that it was one of Walt's first great ideas. I feel it sort of symbolizes Walt's idea of a family friendly, nice, clean amusement park which would be different from all the rest.

Marika, age 12, Heidelberg, Germany

BUZZ LIGHTYEAR'S SPACE RANGER SPIN

Kid Tip
Top Pick

A friendly competition. Buzz Lightyear Space Ranger Spin isn't just a ride; it's a game, too. Shooting lasers at Zurg's targets is lots of fun! It keeps track of your score, so you can compete with your family.

Courtney, age 10,
Williamsburg, VA

Keep shooting those targets. I always beat my mom with the high score. Go for the early shots because these seem to be the most points. Don't stop shooting, even if you don't see any targets.

Brice, age 11, Youngstown, OH

Turn your vehicle for more points. Buzz Lightyear is my favorite ride. There is so much to see. It is different every time so you never get bored. Don't forget that you can turn your car around in circles to try to get even more points.

Adam, age 11, Annapolis, MD

STITCH'S GREAT ESCAPE!

Guard a mischievous Stitch. Stitch's Great Escape is a favorite of mine. Stitch is very funny, and I think it's funny when they show Stitch in the Magic Kingdom at the end. Little kids might get scared because this is the mean Stitch, not the nice one, and it gets dark in the show.

David, age 8, Charleston, MO

MONSTERS, INC. LAUGH FLOOR

Hilarious monster comedians. In the beginning there is a camera that goes around the room finding people from the audience so that a character can say a funny comment about him or her. You feel as if you were at a real comedy show.

Piper, age 12, Carol Stream, IL

Laugh-out-loud (lol) show. You can text in a joke from your parent's phone while you are in the waiting room. The show is very funny and once my joke was used!

Kyle, age 10, Indianapolis, IN

WISHES

Kid Tip
Top Pick

As bright as a star. Wishes are the biggest and the prettiest fireworks. They are so bright it seems like the middle of the day when they are going off.

Nicole, age 11, Braintree, MA

Pick a good spot. Be sure to get a good seat during the fireworks. The ones near the park entrance are best because it's easy to get out, but you can still see the fireworks clearly.

Amanda, age 11, Midlothian, VA

Tinker Bell takes flight. Be sure to pay close attention during Wishes so that you can see Tinker Bell make her flight from the castle!

Ethan, age 10, Pocomoke City, MD

MAIN STREET ELECTRICAL PARADE

Nighttime parade. The Main Street Electrical Parade is a great parade because it has all of the Disney characters lit up with tiny lights. This is a must-see parade that the whole family can enjoy.

Jillian, age 9,
Nova Scotia, Canada

More to Explore

Calling all cowboys. In Frontierland there is a target shooting area. You use quarters and you get so many shots. Things happen when you shoot at the targets. I'd recommend that you start at the front targets because they are easier to shoot and then move to the back ones. It's very fun and interactive.

William, age 12, Stockbridge, MI

Get a Disney haircut. I like to go to the Barber Shop on Main Street to get my hair "colored" with gel, and then they add Mickey Mouse confetti to your hair!! Sometimes they will even paint a Mickey Mouse shape on the back of your head!!

Thomas, age 9, Hilo, HI

Transform into a Princess. I like to go to the Bibbidi Bobbidi Boutique inside the castle. You'll get your own fairy godmother-in-training and you can become a princess. They will do your hair and makeup and you can pick out a dress or bring one from home. It's fun to get dressed up!

Grace, age 7, Carroll, MD

Plunder like a Pirate. Inside Pirates of the Caribbean, there is The Pirates League. You can get made up to look like a real pirate. You'll take a pirate oath and get a new pirate name. It is a lot of fun!

Colin, age 8, Mineola, NY

Meet some of your friends. The best place to see characters is at the Magic Kingdom because the characters are always roaming around somewhere. If you are looking for a certain character, ask a Cast Member; they will tell you when and where they are going to be.

Kellie, age 11, Crete, IL

Explore Cinderella's castle. The thing I love about the Magic Kingdom is the feeling of true happiness and excitement I get when I see Cinderella's castle. Go inside and look at all the pretty pictures on the walls. Some of the tiles they use are made out of real gold!

Rebecca, age 13, Casper, WY

Magical Finds

Talk to a trashcan. Be sure to meet PUSH while you're at the Magic Kingdom! He's usually in Tomorrowland rolling around.

Nathan, age 11, Pittsfield, IL

Call Tinker Bell. See Tinker Bell at Tinker Bell's Treasure—just ask the cast member in the store if you can call Tinker Bell. They will give you a bell to ring and she will come to a magic window.

Elizabeth, age 8, Riva, MD

Make a call to another world. There's a cool looking phone booth by Astro Orbiter. It kind of looks like a rocket. Go inside and press the buttons.   There are a ton of funny phone messages.

Luke, age 11, Jonesborough, TN

Best Places to Eat

Crystal Palace. They serve breakfast, lunch, and dinner and the food is delicious! I went to the breakfast buffet and ate with Winnie the Pooh, Tigger, Piglet and Eeyore. I love that they came to my table one at a time, and you can take your picture with them and get their autograph. It's more personal than when you stand in line to see them. Plus, you get to march in a parade throughout the restaurant with them. It's pretty fun.

Rebeca, age 13, Torrington, CT

Cinderella's Royal Table. Everyone should eat at Cinderella's Royal Table at least once. Being inside the castle felt magical. We went for breakfast, and I loved seeing the princesses. I loved the fruit, bacon, and bread we had. It was cool that they called my parents mi'lord and mi'lady.

Anna, age 10, Stuart, VA

Tony's Town Square. We eat at Tony's every time we visit Disney. I always get a big plate of spaghetti. I also really like that they bring out bread that you can dip in olive oil. I get hungry just thinking about eating here.

Alden, age 15, Stockbridge, MI

Casey's Corner. They serve hot dogs and you can put whatever you want on it—sauerkraut, ketchup, mustard, and cheese sauce. They have really good French fries too.

Braxton, age 10, Prince George, VA

Cosmic Rays. I like to go to Cosmic Rays, but don't go at 6:00 pm or 12:00 pm because it is super packed. They have good chicken fingers and while you eat, you can listen to Sonny, an alien piano player.

> Catherine, age 9,
> Rochester, NY

Pecos Bill. The best place to eat is Pecos Bill. They have great cheeseburgers and there's a bar with all kinds of toppings. You can put anything on your burger!

> Madison, age 10, Omaha, NE

Main Street Bakery. Not everyone knows that the Main Street Bakery has the best cinnamon buns in the world! They are great for breakfast.

> Sarah, age 9, Ontario, Canada

Aloha Isle. Aloha Isle is a great place to get a cool drink or ice cream. I love the Dole Whip! It is very refreshing! It ROCKS!

> Ashleigh, age 9, Littleton, MA

Popcorn Cart. The popcorn is my favorite thing about the Magic Kingdom. It is so tasty; I love to get some before Spectromagic.

> Zane, age 8, Abilene, TX

Epcot

Two parks in one. Epcot feels like two different parks. Future World is made up of buildings with rides that teach you something, but in a fun way. World Showcase is like traveling the world without leaving Florida.

Carley, age 11, Bell, FL

Travel the globe. The people who work in the countries in World Showcase are actually from those countries, so you can ask them questions about where they're from. If you take your autograph book, Cast Members will sign them at the Kidcot spots and write something for you in their language.

Noah, age 11, Cleveland, OH

Try different foods. There are a lot of different foods at Epcot. I ate headcheese and it was really good. I can tell my friends about that to gross them out!

Hannah, age 11, Grand Forks, ND

Use Fastpass in Future World. You won't get to ride Soarin' unless you get a Fastpass. The line is humongous, even early in the day. I'd also try to get a Fastpass for Test Track or Mission Space. Once you've done all the big rides at Epcot, you can relax and walk around World Showcase.

Kevin, age 13, Great Falls, MT

Kids' Vote

Third Favorite Park

Kid Tipsters voted Epcot as their third favorite park.

Top Countries

Mexico, Norway, and Japan are the best countries to visit in World Showcase.

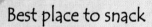

Best place to snack

Epcot is a great place to try different foods from around the globe.

Kid Tip Top Pick

Epcot features 6 Kid Tip Top Pick attractions.

Attraction Ratings

Kid Tipsters voted on each attraction at Walt Disney World. Do you agree with them? Remember you can cast your vote, too! Turn to page 117 to learn how you can become a Kid Tipster.

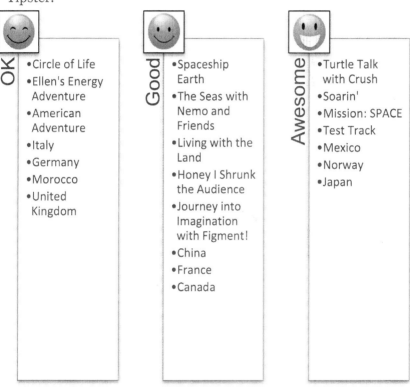

OK
- Circle of Life
- Ellen's Energy Adventure
- American Adventure
- Italy
- Germany
- Morocco
- United Kingdom

Good
- Spaceship Earth
- The Seas with Nemo and Friends
- Living with the Land
- Honey I Shrunk the Audience
- Journey into Imagination with Figment!
- China
- France
- Canada

Awesome
- Turtle Talk with Crush
- Soarin'
- Mission: SPACE
- Test Track
- Mexico
- Norway
- Japan

Attraction Tips

SPACESHIP EARTH

From cave drawings to iPods. You start out in a time machine and you travel back in time to when cavemen lived. They show you the cave drawings that they made to keep records. Then, you see how communication continues until you get to the future.

Bethany, age 10, Camden, NJ

Your future comes to life. The ending of Spaceship Earth is the best! You answer a few questions on the touch screen in front of you, and then using your picture, you get to see what your future might be like. You may go to places by driving your flying car, or maybe into space or under the sea!

Timothy, age 9, Pittsburgh, PA

Interactive games to play. There are the coolest games after you get off Spaceship Earth. I like the driving game and the game where you get what looks like a vacuum and power a city.

Clayton, age 11, Houston, TX

MISSION: SPACE

**Kid Tip
Top Pick**

Train to become an astronaut. Mission Space is a little more extreme, so it might not be good for really little kids, but it is cool! You get to play different roles—Captain, Navigator, Engineer, or Pilot—and you have a job to do during the flight. It is a mission to Mars! There is a more thrilling side and a side for people that don't like spinning.

Austyn, age 14, Charlotte, NC

Blast into outer space. This is my favorite ride at Epcot.   I love the feeling at take off and when you have to take over the controls. I know it is not real; however, I love how real it feels.

Jane, age 10, Owasso, OK

Continue the fun after you ride. The interactive area at the end of Mission Space is great! You compete against other kids on a Mars game. You can even email a video postcard to your friends. There is also a small playground where kids who don't meet the height requirement can play while other members of their family ride the main attraction.

Kyle, age 11, Bristow, VA

ELLEN'S ENERGY ADVENTURE

Energy fuels the universe. Be sure to see this show. It is funny, fun, and you learn a lot about energy. My favorite part is the dinosaur part. The dinosaurs are not as scary as the ones at Animal Kingdom! It's a can't-miss for a first-time visitor.

Ashley, age 12, Holly, MI

TEST TRACK

Kid Tip
Top Pick

Become a crash test dummy. This is one of my family's favorite rides at Epcot! You get to see all the work that goes into making a car safe. Once you get onto the ride, you instantly turn into a crash test dummy. It's a great ride if you like to go fast. My favorite part of the ride is when you actually get out onto the open road.

Samantha, age 13, St. Petersburg, FL

A fun find. When riding Test Track, once in the corrosion chamber, look at the bottom of the robots. They spray you and their IDs spell out CRUS-T and RUS-T.

Max, age 9, Franklin, MA

Add your picture to your card. You can get your ride picture added to your Photopass card. Just ask in the gift shop.

Lindsey, age 11, Hammond, IN

Look for the cool zone near Test Track. It's like a car wash for people.

INNOVENTIONS EAST & WEST

New ideas in technology. Innoventions is a great place to go when you have a lot of time. If you go there once and don't like what you see, don't give up on it—the exhibits are always changing.

Jessica, age 13, Fredericksburg, VA

Cutting-edge, hands-on fun. Make sure you visit Innoventions because you'll see all kinds of technology, from video games to Segways. You can play some very neat, interactive games such as the Great Piggy Bank Adventure or Storm Struck which teaches you things in a fun way.

Tyler, age 11, Morris, IL

THE SEAS WITH NEMO AND FRIENDS

Go under the sea with Nemo. This is a great family ride. I think that it's fun to go around in the little shells, and you get to see Nemo and all of his friends. At the end of the ride, you get

to see Nemo and his dad swimming in the tank with real fish!

Savanah, age 12, Lamar, MO

Inside the pavilion you can get your picture taken inside Bruce's mouth.

TURTLE TALK WITH CRUSH

A totally awesome show. Every kid must see Turtle Talk with Crush, even if they aren't a fan of *Finding Nemo,* the movie. The show is different every time, depending on the people in the audience and the questions asked. It will entertain little kids and adults alike.

Brittney, age 9, Newtown, PA

Talk with a turtle. If a Cast Member picks you, you get to talk into a microphone to Crush and ask him any question you want to! I think it's really cool, and you must stay to the end, even if they don't pick you! He is really funny, DUDE!!

Katie, age 11, Indian Trail, NC

SOARIN'

Kid Tip
Top Pick

Up and away. This ride gives you a little bit of everything. You get a thrill as you're thrust in the air in a hang glider; you experience traveling like never before, and you are exposed to many different landmarks and ideal sightseeing areas.

Maegan, age 9, Langhorne, PA

Smell the fresh air. Soarin' is fantastic! It really feels like you're flying, and it's so interactive, like when you fly over places and you can smell and feel the wind in your hair.

Ross, age 14, Minehead, England

Flying hidden Mickey. I love that Soarin' is in 4D so you can see, smell, hear, and feel all the things on the screen. The orange grove you go over and the views of Yosemite are amazing. Look for the Hidden Mickey on the golf ball!

Elizabeth, age 12, Leeds, AL

LIVING WITH THE LAND

See fish being farmed. Living with the Land is an informative slow boat ride taking you through cool greenhouses where you can learn about various plants. It is very interesting to see the new technology for growing plants and there are some fun objects like Mickey-shaped pumpkins.

Hayden, age 11,
Littleton, MA

You could be eating a tomato grown here. It is really neat to see how life used to be and how things grow, and you get to see how food is grown and used on Disney property. It is neat to see how Disney is helping the planet.

Nicole, age 12, Albany, NY

Tour the greenhouses. We did the Behind the Seeds tour at Epcot and got to touch some of the plants and see how they grow Mickey Pumpkins. The tour lasts about an hour. You can sign up for the tour by Soarin'.

Brice, age 11, Youngstown, OH

THE CIRCLE OF LIFE: AN ENVIRONMENTAL FABLE

Make the world a better place. I like how this movie shows you the effects we are having on the environment, but it is still funny because Timon and Pumbaa are in it. I would get Fastpasses for Soarin' and while you're waiting you can see this movie. It's a great way to cool off and relax for a little bit.

Hunter, age 10, Bradford, IL

Beautiful scenery. This movie reminds me of the Nature movies Disney has made. The screen is very big and the views are awesome! This movie is entertaining for little kids, teens, and grownups.

Jasmine, age 9, Atlanta, GA

JOURNEY INTO IMAGINATION WITH FIGMENT

Tour the Imagination Institute. I like this ride because I have lots of imagination! You see Figment in almost all the scenes. You should plug your nose when Figment becomes a skunk and lets out a big stink! It is the best ride!

Joel, age 7, Flagstaff, AZ

Use your imagination. This ride may sound lame, but it has a whole ton of cool things to do after the ride. I like to do the computer morphing and send the pictures to my friends.

Hannah, age 11, Grand Forks, ND

HONEY, I SHRUNK THE AUDIENCE

Safety Goggles are a must. Honey I Shrunk the Audience is a very funny 3-D movie. Somebody created a shrink ray gun, and it looks like he shrunk everyone in the audience. So he's trying to erase the shrink ray so the audience can be back to our normal size.

Jace, age 8, Whitt, TX

Mice and snakes, oh my! We sometimes skip this movie because there are so many better 3D movies at Disney. Some parts can be scary for younger kids. They have some tails that come out from under the seats and it feels like mice are running around. You will definitely hear screams coming out of the theater.

Michael, age 14, Hudsonville, MI

ILLUMINATIONS: REFLECTIONS FROM EARTH

Lasers and fireworks light up the sky. Illuminations is one of the things you have to see at Epcot. The fireworks and lasers really make the show great. It's also neat how they project images on a World in the center of the lagoon. You can see the fireworks much better from World Showcase than Future World, but it is a lot more crowded.

Dylan, age 14, Andover, NJ

World Showcase

MEXICO

Kid Tip
Top Pick

A grand tour of Mexico. When you go inside the pyramid at Mexico, you feel as if you have entered a Mexican marketplace at nighttime! There are little stands set up with all kinds of souvenirs, and even a boat ride featuring "The 3 Caballeros!"

> Kimberly, age 12,
> Howell, NJ

The stars are always out. I like Mexico because you go inside the pyramid to see the pavilion. It is nice and cool in there, and the scenery is neat. It looks like you are outside at night visiting a marketplace. There is a spot where you can send electronic postcards to your friends.

> Jenna, age 9, Doylestown, PA

Tell Donald hola (hello). You can usually find Donald on the side in his Mexican garb.

> Izzy, age 8, Sheboygan, WI

NORWAY

Kid Tip
Top Pick

Walk around a Norwegian village. Norway is my favorite country. I like the way the workers dress in traditional

Norwegian costumes. I also like the Norway ride filled with trolls. Oh, and the best part: Norway has the best pastries ever!!!!

Kera, age 13, Valdosta, GA

Travel like a Viking. Maelstrom is a boat ride that takes you through a land of magical trolls. At one point you feel like you're going to go down a waterfall, but at the last minute you turn and head in a different direction. It's not that scary and pretty fun. Lots of people skip the movie at the end of the ride, but try to watch it and learn even more about Norway.

Bethany, age 10, Boston, MA

Smile for the troll. I like the trolls in Norway, and my mom always takes a picture of me next to the big troll in the gift shop

area. I have one since I was little and it's funny to see how much I grow each trip.

Payton, age 8,
Deptford, NJ

CHINA

Discover China's beauty. China is my favorite pavilion because there's so much to do. In addition to the Circle-Vision movie, it also has good stores, exhibits, and street performers.

Jessica, age 13
Fredericksburg, VA

Celebrate the Chinese New Year. At the Kidcot station in China, I learned that I was born in the Chinese year of the Dragon and that my brother was born in the year of the Monkey. They told us what that meant and they were really nice.

Kellyn, age 8, Shreveport, LA

GERMANY

It's always Oktoberfest in Germany. I liked Germany and how it was set up like a town square. Try and watch the cuckoo

clock ringing outside. The stores were also really neat, especially the Der Bear store. The statue of the dragon slayer was cool, too.

Jacob, age 11,
Richmond Hill, GA

ITALY

Stop by Venice. I love to walk around Italy. In the back there is a fountain and we always get our picture in front of it. The shops are interesting. It feels like you are really visiting Italy.

Everett, age 11, Syracuse, NY

THE AMERICAN ADVENTURE

Show your pride for the red, white, and blue. Visiting the Unites States pavilion makes me really grateful to be an American and gives me a sense of pride for my country. Watch the show there. It is really good.

Vanessa, age 15, Norwalk, CT

Benjamin Franklin and Mark Twain help bring the story of America to life.

JAPAN

Kid Tip
Top Pick

Tranquil Japan awaits. Japan is in my opinion the greatest themed of all of the countries. It looks incredible. From the Koi ponds to the temple buildings to the restaurants, Japan has everything nicely themed and it's just beautiful.

Tyler, age 14,
Lakeland, FL

Excellent shopping. The Mitsukoshi department store is a great place to shop. You can pick an oyster to get your very own pearl! It has lots of interesting Japanese toys, including Pokémon and Hello Kitty. It also sells Japanese snacks, food, and beverages. Try the marble soda!

Emily, age 10, Montgomery Township, NJ

See candy turned into art. There is a lady from Japan that does demonstrations making animals out of candy. It is really cool! If you wait patiently, she may pick you to choose one of the animals that she will make! You get to keep the candy when she's done.

Ethan, age 10, Pocomoke City, MD

MOROCCO

Beautiful mosaic buildings. I enjoy visiting Morocco. I love looking at the architecture and the details and walking through the buildings. The Mo'Rockin show is fascinating. The music is fun and the belly dancer is engaging and encourages audience participation. There is also a henna artist and the tattoos are beautiful.

Aysia, age 11, Eaton, NY

FRANCE

Stroll along the streets of Paris. You can tell you are in France because of the huge Eiffel Tower. France has the best pastry shop! I love to get an Éclair and sit by the fountain and dream about being in Paris. You can also watch a neat movie called Impressions de France.

Courtney, age 12, Frederick, MD

Eat with a famous chef. I don't know if this happens all the time, but we were able to talk to Remy from *Ratatouille* in the restaurant in France. He comes around on a cart and visits all the tables. He was very funny!

Josh, age 9, Kingsport, TN

UNITED KINGDOM

Just like the real country. My favorite country to visit in World Showcase is the United Kingdom. You can see lots of different characters here. I love to get some fish and chips and then go look at the bears in the toy shop. It is just like I am in the United Kingdom, and I learn a lot about the country too.

Michelle, age 13, Spokane, WA

Soccer rules in the sports shop. I love going to England to see what new soccer items they have for sale in their shops.

Will, age 9, Marietta, GA

Take a picture in a call box. I like to go to England and check out the red phone booths. Sometimes the phone actually rings and there is someone on the other end!

Mitchell, age 10, Johnstown, PA

CANADA

Visit our neighbors to the North. My family and I like Canada the best because of the good places to eat and all of the cool

things that you are able to see there! They have a very good restaurant where you can get pretzel breadsticks. They are delicious!

Caitlyn, age 8, Horseheads, NY

An inspiring movie about Canada. I love the *O Canada* movie. Martin Short is so funny, and it tells you about my own country. I also learn a bit more about my country!

Michael, age 9, Toronto, Canada

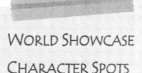

WORLD SHOWCASE
CHARACTER SPOTS
- Donald Duck—Mexico
- Mulan—China
- Snow White & Dopey—Germany
- Aladdin & Jasmine—Morocco
- Belle & Beast—France
- Mary Poppins, Winnie the Pooh, and Alice—United Kingdom

More to Explore

Save the world. I love the Kim Possible missions because you get to use a cool cell phone and search for the bad guys in the World Showcase. The missions are very fun and you feel like a secret spy.

Harley, age 11, Spring Garden, PA

A showcase of characters. The best place to see characters is throughout the countries in World Showcase. The lines didn't seem as long as they did in other parts of Epcot or in other parks. Each country has different characters to meet like Mulan in China and Snow White in Germany.

Hannah, age 8, Lincoln ,NE

Drink soda from around the world. Don't miss Club Cool. You get to drink free soda from around the world. Trick your parents into drinking Beverly—it's awful!

James, age 10, Burlington, NJ

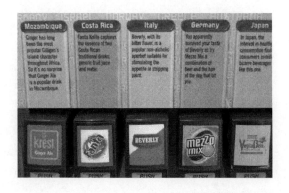

Kidcot Fun Stops. Be sure to get a mask in World Showcase and then go to all the countries and have it stamped. When you get a stamp from all the countries, you get a certificate.

Selah, age 9, Tallahassee, FL

Kidcot Fun Stop in Italy

Jammin' musicians. There are a lot of great musical groups in Epcot. Make sure you see the Jammitors. You can find them in Future World. They play music on trash cans. They are super cool. I also like Off Kilter in Canada. They are really good, even for kids.

Marcus, age 11, Erie, PA

Performances around the World. Take some time to check out the performers. Almost every country has some kind of entertainment. We like to watch the aerobatic kids in China and Sergio the mime in Italy.

Briana, age 13, Red Hook, NY

Hidden Magic

Swirling, sparkling cement. Be sure to see the lighty sidewalks at night near Innoventions.

Leah, age 7, Saint Louis, MO

Play leap frog with water. I love the jumping water outside the Imagination building. I could have fun there forever. It's a great fun way to cool off.

Kaylee, age 10, Sandown, NH

A Coolpost surprise. Look for a place to get drinks between China and Germany. There are a bunch of Coke containers. Lift the lid of one of the containers. I don't want to give the surprise away, but you might feel cooler afterwards.

Dillon, age 9, New Port Richey, FL

Best Places to Eat

Garden Grill. They bring big platters of food to your table and you can eat as little or as much as you want. Something really cool about Garden Grill is, as you eat your food, you are slowly moving in a circle. If you look closely you can see The Land! They served food like chicken and mashed potatoes—your normal country food. The characters there are Pluto, Mickey, and, my personal favorites, Chip 'n' Dale!

Laina, age 10, Ankeny, IA

Coral Reef. At Epcot my favorite place to eat, by far, was the Coral Reef Restaurant. They have a gigantic fish tank with all types of exotic fish swimming around that you can look at while you eat their delicious food. They mostly serve fish, but you can get other items like chicken.

Blake, age 12, Hershey, PA

Biergarten. Other kids will like to eat in Germany because of the buffet. There were a lot of different choices. It's a lot of fun here. There's music playing and they even played a song only using cow bells.

Chloe, age 10, Oakland, MD

Teppan Edo. Be sure to have dinner at Teppan Edo in Japan. The chef makes your food right there in front of you and it is so much fun to watch. They also give you chopsticks to eat with.

Brooke, age 12, Marysville, MI

LeCellier. Canada has the best steak and pretzel bread. They have a dessert called Chocolate Mousse and it really looks like a Moose!!!

Joseph, age 11, Albany, NY

Electric Umbrella. Whenever I am hungry at Epcot, I always ask to go to the Electric Umbrella. The chicken nuggets there are awesome and juicy. It is also one of the only counter service restaurants where you can refill your drink. I also love the fact that it is next to Innoventions!

Lindsey, age 8, Potomac, MD

Sunshine Seasons. A great counter service restaurant at Epcot is Sunshine Seasons. There are many options to choose from, including delicious sandwiches and grilled salmon. It's located in The Land building right next to Living with the Land and Soarin'.

Cory, age 9, Tehachapi, CA

KID TIPSTER WORLD
SHOWCASE FAVORITES

- Churros—Mexico
- School bread—Norway
- Funnel Cakes—American Adventure
- Kaki Gori—Japan
- Éclair—France

Disney's Hollywood Studios

Fast rides and relaxing shows. Hollywood Studios is one of my favorite parks because it has so much for everybody. There are thrill rides, calmer rides, and shows for both kids and adults. Even the decorations around the park make you feel like you're in a movie.

Isabel, age 11, Waymart, PA

The greatest thrills in one park. Hollywood Studios doesn't seem to have as many rides, but the ones they do have are ALL purely awesome! Some of the greatest thrills in all of Walt Disney World are here. Any thrill-lover will go on a frenzy at Hollywood Studios!

Tyler, age 14, Lakeland, FL

Check the time. The shows are really good. Just keep in mind that they only start at certain times so you definitely need to pick up a Times Guide in this park.

Leah, age 12, Norwood, MA

Fastpass Toy Story. You will have to get a Fastpass first thing in the morning for Toy Story Midway Mania if you don't want to wait in a huge line. A lot of times the Fastpasses run out by the afternoon.

Joseph, age 9, Coventry, UK

Kids' Vote

Second Best Park

Kid Tipsters voted the Studios as their second favorite park.

Wild Thrills

Two of the biggest thrill rides—Tower of Terror and Rock 'n' Roller Coaster—are located at the Studios.

Fantasmic Rocks

Kid Tipsters agree that Fantasmic is an awesome nighttime show!

Kid Tip Top Pick

Disney's Hollywood Studios has 5 Kid Tip Top Pick attractions.

Attraction Ratings

Do you agree with the Kid Tipster ratings? You can rate the WDW attractions online at vacationfieldguides.com.

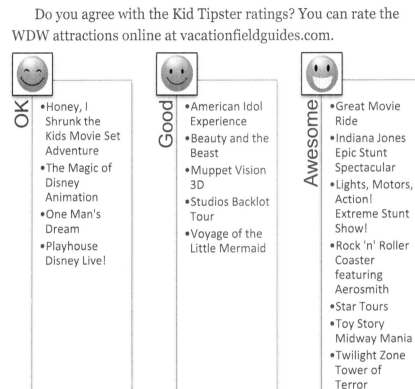

OK
- Honey, I Shrunk the Kids Movie Set Adventure
- The Magic of Disney Animation
- One Man's Dream
- Playhouse Disney Live!

Good
- American Idol Experience
- Beauty and the Beast
- Muppet Vision 3D
- Studios Backlot Tour
- Voyage of the Little Mermaid

Awesome
- Great Movie Ride
- Indiana Jones Epic Stunt Spectacular
- Lights, Motors, Action! Extreme Stunt Show!
- Rock 'n' Roller Coaster featuring Aerosmith
- Star Tours
- Toy Story Midway Mania
- Twilight Zone Tower of Terror

Attraction Tips

THE GREAT MOVIE RIDE

Drive through the movies. The Great Movie Ride is good to go on when you need a break and you want to cool down. You will see scenes from a lot of different movies. My favorite scene is the Wizard of Oz. It's so pretty. There is a surprise during the ride, but I don't want to spoil it. Be prepared you might get robbed, but there is nothing to be scared of.

Zachary, age 8, Battle Creek, MI

Hieroglyphic hidden Mickey. I love the Great Movie Ride because I am a movie buff. It's very fun to see some scenes from movies. Be sure to keep an eye out for the Hidden Mickey in the Indiana Jones scene!

Jennifer, age 12, Leesburg, GA

THE AMERICAN IDOL EXPERIENCE

You could be a star. If you get there early, they might film you and use it in the show. It is really fun! If you're old enough, you could audition to be one of the singers! They will look for singers in the morning.

Erin, age 10, Lewiston, LA

Vote for the final winner. Go to the final show to find out who the grand winner is.

Jerry, age 12, Stratford, CT

INDIANA JONES EPIC STUNT SPECTACULAR

Kid Tip
Top Pick

Indy's greatest movie moments. This is one of the best stunt shows in Disney. If you are a fan of Indiana Jones or other action movies, you will really like it. You sit in a big outdoor theatre. There are lots of really cool stunts. It's like you're on a movie set! If you're lucky, one of your parents might be picked to be an extra!

Taylor, age 12, Omaha, NE

See a director at work. You'll learn how a movie set works and how they switch scenes and do stunts for movies. I loved watching Indy get chased by a giant rock and then fight the bad guys.

Jacob, age 11, Richmond Hill, GA

A practical joke. Near the entrance to the show there is a well with a rope. Pull the rope! It says not to, with the Not crossed out. You'll hear something very funny!

Kerry, age 10, Baltimore, MD

STAR TOURS

Kid Tip
Top Pick

Blast to the Endor Moon. Star Tours is every Star Wars fan's dream. You get to take a trip on a Star Speeder 3000 and it feels like you are really part of a *Star Wars* movie. The ride is a little bumpy in parts.

Michael, age 13,
Cheektowaga, NY

Create your own Light Saber. I made my own Light Saber at the store after the *Star Wars* ride. It was a cool and a fun thing to do. You can also get your picture taken as a *Star Wars* character.

Vance, age 9, Adairsville, GA

MUPPET VISION 3D

The whole family will love it. The Muppet vision 3-D show was amazing! It's cute, funny, and it's in 3-D! I recommend it for all ages! Be sure to stop by and enjoy!

Grace, age 9, Buffalo Grove, IL

Enter the prop warehouse. Everyone will enjoy the pre-show on the TV screens above their heads. Rizzio pretends that he is Mickey Mouse. There is also a ton of Muppet Show props to look at.

Rebecca, age 10, Rochester, NY

Look under the mat. When you enter the building, look to your right. There is a ticket booth with a sign saying the key is under the mat. Lift up the mat on the floor and see what you find!

Angel, age 11, Altona, IL

HONEY, I SHRUNK THE AUDIENCE MOVIE SET ADVENTURE

Towering blades of grass. Everything is super big here. It's fun to play on the big ant. Be careful of the super-sized super soaker. Sometimes water squirts out of it.

Drew, age 8, Bay Area, CA

LIGHTS, MOTORS, ACTION! EXTREME STUNT SHOW

Intense action and effects. Be sure to make it to Lights, Motors, Action! The show is amazing! It's loud, people jump off of buildings, and you really feel the hot fire, but don't be too worried none of it happens to you.

Tara, age 11, Omaha, NE

Movie stunts explained. Don't miss this stunt show! If you love fast cars and cool stunts, this is the show for you. It feels like you are watching a real movie being made.

Michael, age 10, Kenner, LA

STUDIO BACKLOT TOUR

Step inside a movie. I like the Backlot Tour because of the many things it offers. You get to watch people participate in a skit (if you're lucky, it might be one of your family members) and learn secrets about the film industry. You also get to ride in a tram and see behind the scenes at the Studios. At the end, you can explore a small museum with costumes from Disney movies.

Shawn, age 14, Ethel, LA

Backstage sneak peek. You might be able to see the drivers from Lights, Motors, Action! Extreme Stunt Show performing or rehearsing. I got to see them rehearsing once and it was really cool to see behind the scenes.

Olivia, age 11, Maple Valley, WA

Become part of the movie action. I like when they take you back where there is a big truck and they make it explode and the fire comes down and water rushes all around you. You think you're going to get soaked, but you don't really!

Natalie, age 10, Crown Point, IN

Look for larger-than-life movie set props right outside the Studio Backlot Tour.

TOY STORY MIDWAY MANIA
Kid Tip
Top Pick

Shrink to the size of a toy. The ride is a mix of Buzz Lightyear's Space Ranger Spin, a carnival game, and a 3D version of the movie *Toy Story*. You get to do a ring toss, a shooting arcade, and a balloon pop. It's a blast! You'll want to be sure to get to the park early just for this ride!

Matthew, age 9, Tyler, TX

Better than any video game. Toy Story Mania is my favorite ride. Being a teenager, you may think it is babyish because of *Toy Story*, but it is even better than any video game played at home. Sometimes when you shoot a target, air or water will shoot out at you (but not a lot of water!).

Kevin, age 13, Cheektowaga, NY

Interactive Mr. Potato Head. I like looking at all the humongous toys in the line area. For example, the lights are

gigantic Christmas tree lights held up with huge tinker toys. If you use the Fastpass line, you will not get to see Mr. Potato Head, but the Fastpass is so worth it because the lines get super long.

McKenna, age 10,
West Palm Beach, FL

WALT DISNEY: ONE MAN'S DREAM

It all started with Walt. I would be sure to tell other kids to visit Walt Disney: One Man's Dream because it is a great way to learn about the person who created Disney World. It is all about Walt Disney's life. The attraction ends with a video about Walt with actual video of what he did.

Emily, age 12, South Hackensack, NJ

See a dream come to life. I always love to stop by and see One Man's Dream. You get to walk through and see some models and even Walt's desk. You can skip the movie at the end, but I don't recommend that. Everyone should learn about the man who taught us all how to dream.

Ariel, age 11, Westfield, MA

VOYAGE OF THE LITTLE MERMAID

Go under the sea with Ariel. I like that there are real people in this show. Ariel is a real girl and she sings the songs from the movie. The other characters are puppets. The sea witch is scary looking. I like how the main idea is conveyed in less than 30 minutes.

Larisa, age 9, Billings, MT

Get carried away. You might not want to sit in the front rows because a big wave will come and you will get misted with water. It's not a lot of water, but my dad's glasses got all wet.

Julie, age 11, Glen Ridge, NJ

THE MAGIC OF DISNEY ANIMATION

See a pencil drawing turn into animation. There are two parts to The Magic of Disney Animation. First you'll see a funny show about how a character is created. Then you can learn to draw a Disney character at the Animation Academy. We drew a lot that day. My favorite character to draw was Tinker Bell, but she was really hard to do.

Ashley, age 8, Moline, IL

Spot unusual characters. Sometimes, when you are waiting for the animation class, the place fills up with characters that you don't normally see, like the villains.

Noelle, age 9, Sheboygan, WI

A picture worth framing. I could have stayed there all day. We learned how to draw Pluto, Goofy, Dale, and Tinker Bell. It was really fun and makes a great souvenir. When we came home we framed all of our drawings and they mean a lot to us.

Lexi, age 10, Rochester, NY

Create art with an Imagineer. I really like the Magic of Disney Animation. I got to sit in a real artist's chair. A Disney animation artist teaches you how to draw step by step, so it is really hard to mess up. I think all the kids should do this because it is a free souvenir and because if it wasn't for drawing Disney characters there would be no Disney World.

Delaney, age 9, Concord, NH

PLAYHOUSE DISNEY—LIVE ON STAGE!

Celebrate with Disney pals. Playhouse Disney Live has a lot of characters in it. There is Handy Manny, my friends Tigger and Pooh, and even Minnie and Mickey. If you sit too close to the stage, you can't see the whole show very well. If you sit in the middle, you get to grab bubbles and streamers that shoot out into the audience. Even if you go in right before they close the doors you can see a lot.

Luke, age 5, Arlington, VA

Great for little kids. This show was awesome when I was a little kid. It's just ok now, but little kids will love it.   It has some characters from the Disney TV shows.

Joey, age 8, Holbrook, NY

BEAUTY AND THE BEAST—LIVE ON STAGE

A tale as old as time. I love all the songs in this play. It's like the movie, but there is more dancing. The costumes are very colorful and any *Beauty and the Beast* fan should definitely check this out. The theater is very big, so I'd tell kids to get there early so you can have a seat closer to the front.

Erin, age 10, Laguna Beach, CA

The perfect spot to wait. Grab a Fastpass for Rock 'n' Roller Coaster, then go see the show. When the show is finished, it will probably be time for you to ride!

Todd, age 12, Wilmington, DE

ROCK 'N' ROLLER COASTER
Kid Tip
Top Pick

Rockin' Aerosmith music. Rock 'N' Roller Coaster is a very fun ride and the music is great! You meet up with Aerosmith at the recording studio and then you're off to a premier in a super stretch limo. You go at an unbelievable speed upside down, rockin' out to music in the stereo behind your head.

Justin, age 13, Tyler, TX

Launch at super fast speeds. The ride goes from 0 to 60 miles per hour in about 2 seconds. That's amazing! The ride is so neat because it's dark and you can't really tell where you're going. It also has three loops, which is crazy! You go through donuts, the "O" in Hollywood, and much more!

Matthew, age 10, St. Louis, MO

Keep your eyes open wide. I really like riding in the back because it seems even faster. You should always try to smile at the very beginning because that is when they take your picture, and you should always keep your eyes open or you will not see all the neon signs.

Madison, age 12, Goldsboro, NC

Speed through the single rider line. Get there early so that way you won't have to wait in line much. They also have a single rider line here, so if you want to come back and don't mind riding alone, you can get in that line and it goes fast.

Kayla, age 11, Simi Valley, CA

THE TWILIGHT ZONE TOWER OF TERROR

Kid Tip
Top Pick

Intense drop sequence. I think the Tower of Terror is great and really intense. It is extremely nerve racking and may even frighten younger children. You get to walk through what seems like an old hotel. The way they present the story is great! I felt like I not only plunged into the movie, but into the Twilight Zone!

MacKenzie, age 13,
Hicksville, NY

Thrill-seekers only. The ride might seem like a nice slow ride, but the next thing you know—BAM you rise up and fall back down! It is an action-packed adventure that is different every time.

Garrison, age 10, Payne, OH

A great time waiting in line. I rode Tower of Terror for the first time this year and really enjoyed all of the things in the queue. There are a lot of cool things to look at. Try to find a hidden Mickey in the library. Who thought waiting in line could be fun?

Emily, age 13, Vacherie, LA

FANTASMIC

Not just fireworks. Fantasmic is more of a show than just fireworks. There are these huge water screens and they project movie scenes on them. You'll also see Mickey defeat the bad villains and even battle a dragon. The ending is awesome!

A.J., age 12, Hugo, MN

A fantastic nighttime show. Fantasmic is the best show ever! We never miss it. If you are a fan of Disney villains, you will be happy to see this show! The theater is huge and sometimes the audience starts up the wave before the show starts.

Marie, age 11, Albuquerque, NM

Can be scary. Fantasmic might scare little kids. If you're a little bit afraid of loud noises, sit towards the back.

Katie, age 7, Indianapolis, IN

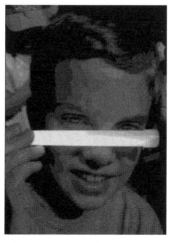

Goofing around before Fantasmic

More to Explore

Train to be a Jedi. The Jedi Training is great! You get to battle Darth Vader and get a certificate at the end. I didn't get picked the first time, but then went back and was jumping up and down and got picked. It was cool!

Ryan, age 9, Emerson, NJ

Block Party Bash. The Block Party parade at Hollywood Studios is my favorite parade in Disney. There is so much energy, dancing and singing, which I really love. The characters jump on trampolines, use jump ropes, and hula hoops.

Hayden, age 8, Woodland Park, CO

Character spots all around. Look for all the hidden character spots around the park. We were able to meet Lightning McQueen and Mater and Sorcerer Mickey Mouse.

Maya, age 9, Brentwood, TN

Magical Finds

Hollywood is full of performers. Take some time to watch the many street performers. They are always hilarious and sometimes they pick kids out of the audience to be part of the show!

Noah, age 14, Dania, FL

Funny hand prints. Outside the Great Movie Ride is a bunch of handprints and footprints in cement from famous Disney people. It's fun to walk around and see all the names.

Adam, age 8, Bellevue, WA

Singing in the rain. In the Streets of America part of the park, there is an umbrella. Pull the umbrella, but make sure you're under it first!

Jessica, age 8, Wingate, NC

Best Places to Eat

50's Prime Time Café. 50's Prime Time is a great place to
have a casual lunch or dinner. The
entire restaurant is decked out like a
kitchen from the 1950s! The staff
treats you like family and will even
ask you to keep your elbows off the
table. One time the waitress made
my mom stand in the corner because
she didn't eat all of her vegetables! It
was very funny to watch! The PB & J
shakes are the best!

Jason, age 14, Moore, OK

Sci-Fi Drive in Theater. Kids should totally eat at the Sci-Fi
Diner!! You get to sit in your very own car and eat dinner. Your
mom and dad sit in the backseat and you get to sit in the front
where you can see the drive in movie screen. The food is great!
I get a hamburger and a sundae for dessert. My mom and dad
like it because it is a nice quiet place to eat after a long day.

Delaney, age 9, Concord, NH

Pizza Planet Arcade. Pizza Planet is a
pizza place and a giant arcade. They
have the best pizza in WDW.

Rocco, age 12,
Pennsauken, NJ

Disney's Animal Kingdom

All kinds of animals. I love all the animals at Animal Kingdom! Most of them are very interesting. There are Cast Members around that tell you cool facts about them. There is a wide range of animals—Komodo dragons, gorillas, okapis, even naked mole rats!

Katie, age 10, Indian Trail, NC

Have your camera ready. When you are at Animal Kingdom, be sure to go on the animal treks. There are various ones throughout the park, and they have many beautiful and sometimes exotic animals that you can't help but stare at. Don't forget your camera!

Jakiee, age 15, Sparta, NJ

Slow down and look around. Animal Kingdom is a park where you have to take things slowly and look around. If you rush from ride to ride, you're going to miss some awesome stuff.

Micah, age 11, Vacherie, LA

Get a Fastpass to see the Yeti. Expedition Everest is the coolest ride at Animal Kingdom. Get a Fastpass right away. If you want to ride again, you can use the single rider line.

Elijah, age 8, Rochelle Park, NJ

Kids' Vote

Rated Fourth

Kid Tipsters love thrill rides, but Animal Kingdom only has a couple.

Great Entertainment

You'll find a lot of authentic entertainment and hidden finds at Animal Kingdom.

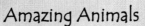

Amazing Animals

Take some time to see all the incredible wildlife.

Kid Tip Top Pick

There are 4 Kid Tip Top Pick attractions.

Attraction Ratings

OK

- Conservation Station
- Flights of Wonder
- Primeval Whirl
- TriceraTop Spin

Good

- Rafiki's Planet Watch
- Affection Section
- The Boneyard
- Discovery Island Trails
- It's Tough to Be a Bug
- Pangani Forest Exploration Trail

Awesome

- Dinosaur
- Expedition Everest
- Festival of the Lion King
- Finding Nemo: The Musical
- Kali River Rapids
- Kilimanjaro Safaris
- Maharajah Jungle Trek

Attraction Tips

THE OASIS

Keep your eyes open. Take your time walking through the Oasis—you'll miss something if you don't. My family and I saw birds laying on eggs when we went the first time.

Amy, age 9, Pennsville, NJ

IT'S TOUGH TO BE A BUG!

Bugs have feelings too! This movie is great! You get to travel under the Tree of Life. Make sure you check out all the cool carvings in the tree. Once you enter the theater, you get a pair of "bug eyes" to wear. Make sure you read the posters while you're waiting for the movie. They are very funny.

Jessica, age 11, Mexico City, Mexico

Cool special effects. If you like the movie *A Bug's Life*, you will like this 3D movie. It is kind of scary, but funny too! The best part is when they spray the bug spray at you; it makes your shoelaces glow!

Lindsey, age 10, Shelbyville, TN

Pick your seat carefully. The sounds and bugs can be scary for younger kids. You may not want to sit in the front row if you get scared easily. Hopper is scary in the front.

Gracie, age 8, West Warwick, RI

DISCOVERY ISLAND TRAILS

Animals to discover. Discovery Island Trails are fun because you can read the information about the animals to learn about them. There are also different animals there than in the rest of the park. I love the lemurs and kangaroos.

Alex, age 10, Gardner, KS

FESTIVAL OF THE LION KING
Kid Tip
Top Pick

Broadway-quality show. The show is very good. All of the actors dress up in really cool costumes like the ones from the Broadway show. My favorite song is "Can you feel the love tonight" because they have two people, dressed as birds, fly around the stage! It is really cool.

Molly, age 12, Waxhaw, NC

Action-packed performance. The Festival of the Lion King show is really neat. We see it every time we go and it's always good. It's just the right length so that you cool off and enjoy the show, but don't get bored. My favorite part of the show is the Tumble Monkeys—they are great.

John Carter, age 9, Hoover, AL

Fun for all ages. The show features circus-level acrobatics, a different story line than the *Lion King* movies, and they choose people from the audience to dance and sing. It's entirely appropriate for all ages.

Chase, age 12, Scappoose, OR

KILIMANJARO SAFARIS

Kid Tip
Top Pick

A wild jungle adventure. Kilimanjaro Safaris was an awesome ride. The tour guide takes you for a ride in a jeep-type vehicle

and stops along the way to let you view different animals. Every ride is different because you never know when the animals will appear or what they will be doing. We got to watch some elephants playing in the water on our last trip. It was really funny.

Jocelyn, age 11, Ontario, Canada

Rescue an elephant. Kilimanjaro Safaris is another don't-miss ride for kids and adults of all ages. It is incredible to see all the animals and the story of the poachers is a lesson for everyone to learn.

Connor, age 10,
Highlands Ranch, CO

Visit first thing. Go early in the morning so the animals are moving around—if you go when it's really hot during the day, they're mostly lying around.

Shanna, age 9, Gilbert, SC

PANGANI FOREST EXPLORATION TRAIL

Become a researcher and track animals. The trails might look boring, but they are a lot of fun. I recommend you pick up a bird guide in the bird room. It will help you identify all the different birds. The meerkats and the gorillas are my favorite.

Eddy, age 14,
Roaring Springs, PA

RAFIKI'S PLANET WATCH

See animals up close. Rafiki's Planet Watch and Conservation Station is fun. You get to see animals and maybe even touch

one, like a lizard. There are animal cutouts to get your pictures taken with, and there are also characters signing autographs. We saw Jiminy Cricket and Pocahontas. There are all kinds of animal activities and outside you can pet farm animals.

Riley, age 8, Indianapolis, IN

Watch a Veterinarian work. If you go early, you may even see the vets operating on an animal!

Payton, age 8, Deptford, NJ

FLIGHTS OF WONDER

Swooping, soaring birds. This is an awesome show that a lot of people don't seem to know about or take the time to see. You are entertained by all kinds of birds that you would not normally see. There are even some endangered birds. They get the audience involved, and have the birds fly right over you. A must-see for anyone who loves birds.

> Quentin, age 13,
> Crown Point, IN

Bird lovers only. This show is kind of goofy, but a nice break from walking! You learn about birds of prey. If you're afraid of birds, this is not the show for you. They fly out over the audience! My grandma had to run out during the show!

> Natalie, age 15, North Carolina

MAHARAJAH JUNGLE TREK

A wild jungle trail. Be sure to see the Asian tigers. Unlike most exhibits, these tiger cats are always roaming around. They also have a large area.

> Laura, age 10, Jupiter, FL

KALI RIVER RAPIDS

Kid Tip
Top Pick

A wet, wild ride. I like Kali River Rapids because, not only is it a fun water raft ride and a great way to cool off, it tells the story of how logging can destroy our environment. It goes along great with the themes of Animal Kingdom.

Carly, age 11, Worcester, MA

Squirt other riders. After you are done with the ride, you can go on the bridge on the way out and press buttons to make elephants squirt water on the people on the ride! It's so much fun!

Taytem, age 11, Deptford, NJ

Not as busy during the parade. Sometimes when it is not too crowded, they will let you ride over and over without getting off. So go in the early morning or during a parade.

Madison, age 12, Goldsboro, NC

FINDING NEMO THE MUSICAL

High-flying musical fish. My favorite show is Finding Nemo the Musical. It is so cool to see all the characters come to life, especially the pelican and Crush. The show seems different from the movie because of all the new songs. Some of the characters even come off the stage!

Josh, age 9, Chicago, IL

EXPEDITION EVEREST

Kid Tip
Top Pick

Thrilling train ride. Expedition Everest is such a fun ride with a neat story behind it. As you enter the queue, you instantly become part of the journey to the Himalayan Mountains to search for the terrifying, immensely-feared Yeti. There are a lot of surprises—you go backwards and even encounter the Yeti!

Haley, age 13, Clarion, PA

A queue worth seeing. Make sure that you experience the whole line at least once without using Fastpass or single rider. The line itself is an attraction. It's like walking through a cool museum.

Kelly, age 12, Brookfield, WI

Even scarier when the sun goes down. The ride is even better when you ride it at night because it makes it scarier!

Michael, age 13, Cheektowaga, NY

BONEYARD

Uncover a woolly mammoth. The boneyard is great—it's a big playground where there are really high slides, climbing nets, and you can even dig for dinosaur bones!

Niamh, age 8, Glasgow, Scotland

Caves to explore and things to climb. I like to explore the caves and take pictures with the dinosaur fossils. I can dig for hours for dinosaur bones. The sand is neat and doesn't stick to your hands.

Indigo, age 6, Eaton, NY

PRIMEVAL WHIRL

A spinning trip through time. In Dinoland, there is a spinning ride called Primeval Whirl. It takes you through the time when dinosaurs disappeared in a cartoon version. This ride can get you really dizzy. Your "time machine" spins, drops, and goes pretty high. If you get sick or don't enjoy spinning, I wouldn't go on this ride!

Emily, age 9, Leander, TX

A mini roller coaster. Primeval Whirl is a lot of fun! It has many spins and turns that whip you around and around! Your parents might want to sit this one out.

Michael, age 13, Warner Robins, PA

TRICERATOP SPIN

Soaring dinos. This ride is a nice ride for the younger kids to go on while the older kids go on Primeval Whirl. You sit in a dinosaur and can go up and down. It is like Dumbo at the Magic Kingdom.

Richie, age 10, Alburtis, PA

DINOSAUR

Rescue a dinosaur. Dinosaur is a lot of fun! You board a time rover vehicle and travel back in time to find a dinosaur. It can

be scary in some parts. The dinosaurs look very real! I wouldn't recommend it for younger kids. But if you like to be scared, you'll like this ride!

Rachel, age 10,
Portland, OR

A bumpy ride full of some close calls. Dinosaur is the scariest ride I've ever been on. The first time I rode it I thought it was going to be lame. Not at all! It's kind of bumpy, dark, and loud. Don't worry; nothing bad will happen to you. Don't forget to look at your picture at the end.

Joshua, age 11, Jackson, MO

A cool gift shop. The Dinosaur gift shop is awesome! Even if you don't ride the ride, you should check out the gift shop.

Maxwell, age 10, Riva, MD

More to Explore

Places to explore. Pick up The Kids' Discover Club card. You can do different activities at marked spots, and the Cast Members stamp your card at each spot. At the end you get a prize.

Rachel, age 10,
Cape Cod, MA

Safari characters. Don't forget to go to Camp Minnie-Mickey to meet your favorite characters. They are all dressed in safari outfits.

Maddi, age 9, Houston, TX

Mickey's Jammin' Jungle Parade. Definitely stay for the parade here! It is very entertaining. Also, don't rush through this park because there is a lot to see while here!

Seth, age 15, Knoxville, TN

Tree of Life. The thing I like best about Animal Kingdom is the

Tree of Life. I love to explore the tree and see all the different animals carved into the tree.

Jordan, age 11, Bell, FL

The Tree of Life has 325 animals carved into it.

Magical Finds

Dance in Africa. I love the African dancers. You can dance with them and not feel silly. The people that work there are so nice. I had so many questions about Africa and they answered every one.

Julianna, age 9, Great Falls, MT

Keep an eye out for street performers. They can do some really interesting things. For example, one time they did the limbo and I can't even describe how low he went!

Caroline, age 12, Exeter, NH

Take a break in Asia. In Asia, there's a monkey enclosure on a small island. The monkeys are very funny to watch, and convenient if you just want to relax and take a break from the rides.

Jessica, age 13,
Fredericksburg, VA

Look for DeVine. She is a woman who is dressed like a large green tree branch. You have to look carefully because she really blends into the bushes and trees! But she does come out onto the sidewalk and moves around.

Joey, age 9, Kenilworth, NJ

Watch the acrobats. There are some cool acrobats that perform in front of that bar near the Harambe entrance. They can do some really cool and interesting things.

Andrew, age 12, Buffalo, NY

Try to find Wes Palm. He's a taking palm tree! I wore a palm-tree-covered Hawaiian shirt one year and he was all over me saying I was wearing his family tree!

Nicolas, age 11, Murry, KY

Working on the Animal Kingdom Safari Journal.

Best Places to Eat

Tusker House. If you get a really early reservation at Tusker House, you can be in the park before it opens. It's a buffet. There are fruit, bagels, doughnuts, cereal, eggs, potatoes, bacon, and sausage. They bring jungle juice to your table—it's awesome! You can meet Donald, Daisy, Mickey, and Goofy. We played music and danced around and had lots of fun.

Olivia, age 9, Toledo, OH

Flame Tree Barbecue. The food here is very yummy. You can sit near the pond while you eat. My dad likes the ribs, and my mammy has pulled pork. They have fruit plates and frozen lemonade.

Alexander, age 8, Durham, England

Picnic in the Park. The picnic in the park is the best. You get your bag of food and then get to eat it anywhere you want. You can even get macaroni and cheese and a big brownie or giant rice krispie treat. There are picnic tables all over the park.

Dominique, age 10, Pekin, IL

Pizzafari. I love the pizza at Pizzafari! You get your own individual pizza. The rooms you sit in are very colorful and full of animals. Even the chairs have animals on them!

Weston, age 11, Cincinnati, OH

Water Parks

The water parks are fun for the whole family—featuring fast speed slides, lazy raft rides, and even a kid's play area. So take a break from the parks and spend the afternoon playing in the Florida sunshine. Just don't forget your sunscreen!

Don't skip the water parks. A lot of people skip the water parks, but they are SO much fun. We make sure to go there early in the day or later in the afternoon because lunch time seems to be the busiest.

Noah, age 10, Linwood, NJ

Almost as big as a theme park. The water parks are humongous! Much bigger than the indoor water parks by my house.

Ben, age 7, Merrimack, NH

Rent a towel and locker. You can rent pool towels at each of the water parks. It is much easier to do this than to bring them from your hotel. We also rent a small locker to keep our stuff in so that it doesn't get lost.

Steven, age 13, Woodbridge, VA

Sunscreen is a must. Don't forget to reapply your sunscreen so you don't get burned. Disney is no place to be burned and miserable.

Morgan, age 9, Montreal, Canada

The pavement gets hot. Be sure to bring goggles and water shoes. The goggles are good for the wave pool and some lifeguards will let you wear them on the slides. I always wear water shoes so I can get to all the slides quicker, and I don't burn my feet!

Sydney, age 11, Clarence, NY

Sweet mini-treats. There are yummy mini-donuts that are only available at the water parks. They are delicious!

Andrew, age 8, Brea, CA

Try swimming in the rain. Go to the water parks in the rain. Unless it's lightening or raining so hard the lifeguards can't see the pool bottom, the parks are open. We went to Typhoon Lagoon during a tropical storm and had a blast! There were hardly any people in the park, so we could do whatever we wanted with no wait. Hey, you're going to get wet anyhow!

Brittany, age 10, Fairfield County, CT

TYPHOON LAGOON

Super big waves. The wave pool is awesome! Just be careful not to get any scratches off the bottom of the pool. It is really rough.

Aaron, age 12, Manchester, United Kingdom

Play in the sand. At Typhoon Lagoon you can ride the slides and take a break and build castles in the sand. I also love the lazy river.

Sierra, age 8, Melbourne, FL

Cool water coasters. Crush 'n' Gusher is awesome! You can go on either a two-person or three-person raft. The line is usually shorter for the three-person rafts, so find two friends if you can. This ride is different from other rides because water jets push you up some of the hills as well as down the slide parts. You also get some cool pictures coming out of the tube at the bottom because there's usually a photographer there.

Bailey, age 14, Pittsburgh, PA

Circle the entire park. Take a break from the slides and float along the lazy river. It's fun and you can circle the whole park to see what else you might want to go on.

Marissa, age 9, Washington, D.C.

Speed down Humunga Kowabunga. This is the biggest slide at Typhoon Lagoon! You zoom out of the tube going super fast! Go on this slide first because the lines can get super long.

Cody, age 12, Fall River, MA

Swim with Sharks. You can snorkel with fish and sharks! The sharks are kind of tiny and don't bite. You can only swim across once, and then you have to get out. It is super cool seeing the fish up close. You can use an underwater camera to take pictures.

Rick, age 11, Kenilworth, NJ

BLIZZARD BEACH

Cool kids' meals. When you eat at Blizzard Beach, you get a sand bucket and shovel. We didn't do this till after we were done, but I wish we had eaten first so I could use the bucket to play with.

> Maddi, age 7,
> Chillicothe, OH

Brave the Summit. Blizzard Beach is the best water park because there is an awesome speed slide called Summit Plummet that shoots you straight down and it looks like you are going to fly off a ski lift. It's the world's tallest and fastest slide!

> Amy, age 9, Linden, MI

Ski on floating ice. I liked the Ski Patrol Training Camp! It's cool to zip down the zip line and walk across icebergs, just remember to stay balanced or you'll fall into the water!

> Garrett, age 11, Plainville, CT

Try the family raft ride. My family loves to go on Teamboat Springs. Your whole family sits in a giant circle raft. Even my grandma likes this ride. You have to have more than two people to go on this slide, so don't get in line if there are just two of you. They take your picture, too.

> Cole, age 10, Freehold, NJ

Downtown Disney

Don't miss Downtown Disney. There are many things for kids to do, and it's a great place to get souvenirs. There are awesome shops, pin trading, and food. It's not like your average downtown. Everything here is Disney.

Splash Zones. Stitch spits at you from the top of the World of Disney store. That was funny. There are some fun water spouts to play in, too.

> Haileigh, age 7,
> Norman, OK

Disney Quest. Disney Quest is a fun, interactive place to go to with a bunch of virtual reality games. You can create your own roller coasters, songs, and cartoon characters! Beware of the dinosaurs on the virtual raft ride! There are also some swashbuckling pirates to watch out for. It is fun to go here on a rainy day or to take a break from the parks.

> Shawn, age 10, Rochester, MN

Pin Traders. If you collect pins, they have the Pin Traders Store and sometimes they have people outside with their pin collections that you can trade with.

> Anthony, age 13, Boise, ID

Life-size Lego sculptures. The coolest thing in Downtown Disney, I have to say, is all of the Lego sculptures. The dragon in the water is one of my favorites, but the dogs are pretty cool too.

Lydia, age 15,
Evansville, IN

Lego Imagination Center. You can buy bricks and create your own Lego people. You can also build your own race car and race it against other kids. Last year I got an Indiana Jones set. You can never have too many Legos.

Nate, age 11, Potomac, MD

Mickey's Mart. There are lots of stores to shop in! I like the $10 or less store. I can buy stuff with my own money there and it's just fun to look around at all the Disney stuff.

Laura, age 9, Hockessin, DE

Once Upon a Toy. They have a toy store where you can fill a box with Mr. Potato head or My Little Pony stuff. You can get

Buzz Lightyear and Mary Poppins stuff for your potato head. If you don't have to buy the potato, there is more room in your box for toys.

Brandon, age 8, Margate, FL

World of Disney. World of Disney is the largest Disney store on Earth! You can find everything there, so you don't have to stop in the gift shops in the parks. There are rooms and rooms of Disney stuff. The store is so big you could get lost in it! They also have the Bibbidi Bobbidi Boutique in the girl section of the store. You can get made up to look like a princess or a rock star.

Jasmine, age 12, Cleveland, OH

Team Mickey. You can buy ESPN and other sports stuff at Team Mickey. One year, I got a custom-made baseball! I really want a custom bat, but those are more expensive. If you're lucky, you can see the bat guy make the bats out of a block of wood.

Logan, age 10, Newport, NE

Design-A-Tee. For my birthday last year, I got to design my very own tee shirt. There are a ton of characters to choose from. There are even sayings you can write on your shirt. It takes about an hour for them to make the shirt, so do this first thing when you get to Downtown Disney. I got a lot of special attention from Cast Members when I wore my birthday shirt.

Sam, age 8, Chicago, IL

T-Rex. The dinosaur restaurant has cool dinosaurs and a squid to look at while you eat. They also have a place where you can dig for bones and make build-a-dinosaurs. The kid smoothies come in bone cups! The gift shop is cool, too.

Lila, age 7, Pierceton, IN

Earl of Sandwich. Make sure to visit the Earl of Sandwich and try their Pizza Sandwich. It is delicious! They have lots of different sandwiches to try.

Isaiah, age, 11, Riva, MD

Ghirardelli Soda Fountain & Chocolate Shop. Be sure to go to Ghirardelli Chocolates for a free taste of chocolate!

Katelyn, age 9, Murray, KY

Goofy's Candy Co. Check out Goofy's Candy Company. I like the candy tubes and make-your-own candy-dipped pretzels. They will put any topping you want on them. It is so messy, but delicious.

Alyssa, age 12, Milton, FL

KID TIPSTERS
FAVORITE SOUVENIRS
• Tee shirts
• Lego toys
• Disney stuffed animals
• Mr. Potato Head pieces
• Pins
• Key chains
• Mouse Ears
• Build your own light saber

Disney Resorts

From larger-than-life Disney characters to free roaming animals, each Disney resort has its own special theme. Staying at a Disney resort is sure to be fun!

All-Star Music. Kids who like music will really like this hotel. There are music notes and huge instruments all around. It's very colorful and the rooms are comfortable. Look for the very large cowboy boots. They have Mickey heads on them.

Alexis, age 12, Birmingham, AL

All-Star Movies. I really liked the Toy Story building at the All-Star Movies the best. The stairs are inside the Bucket of Toy Soldiers! Some of the toy soldiers are on top of the building! The rooms are bright and the best pool is the one with Sorcerer Mickey.

Nicole, age 11, Davenport, FL

All-Star Sports. All-Star Sports is my favorite because I like sports. It also has a cooler pool. The baseball pool is the best. It has a football field with Xs and Os that are so fun to run through. Every day I would run through on my way to breakfast.

Jace, age 8, Whitt, TX

Pop Century. When you first start to pull in, there are funny signs to read. In the lobby, there are framed displays from the 50s though the 90s. It's fun because of all the oversized toys they have there. My favorite was the huge Hot Wheels bike. It's just a different resort that you can't see anywhere other than Disney!

Ben, age 9, Philadelphia, PA

Caribbean Beach. We liked the pirate rooms at Caribbean Beach. You can store juices and fruit in your fridge and it's shaped like a barrel. If you take a walk to the pirate pool, you might see a lot of birds and animals. We rode a surrey bike around the lake and took out a paddle boat. The pirate  pool is great. It has two slides and a boat in it.

Catherine, age 9, Rochester, NY

Coronado Springs. I love the Mexican theming—even the vending machines match! I enjoy just walking around the resort and looking at all the details. At the Dig Site you'll find the pyramid pool with a big water slide, and there's also a playground for little kids. The rooms are very nice and the beds are comfy. You'll be glad you're coming back here after the parks.

Kylie, age 14, Omaha, NE

Ft. Wilderness. We stayed in a cabin at Fort Wilderness one year. It was my favorite trip. My Dad rented a golf cart and we drove all around the resort. We went fishing one day and I caught my first fish. My only problem was that the pool was kind of boring. But I still had fun swimming. I got to sleep in a bunk bed. That was fun. I like to go tent camping. But this was fun, too, and we had our own bathroom.

Will, age 10, Corinth, TX

Port Orleans Riverside. I like the Alligator Bayou section. It feels more secluded and it's nice to look around at all the scenery. You can take a boat from the resort to Downtown Disney. You can even have your hair braided. Look for the stand by the river.

Alicia, age 12, Northport, AL

Port Orleans French Quarter. French Quarter was my favourite. When you come in and out of the resort, they give you doubloons to throw in the wishing fountain. They have really good pin trading at night. You can take a boat to Downtown Disney. They have jazz music at night. The pool is not too big, but they have a water slide. It feels  like you're in New Orleans. They have really good beignet snacks at the restaurant.

Liam, age 9, Nova Scotia, Canada

Animal Kingdom Lodge and Villas. If you love animals, you will love Animal Kingdom Lodge. It's so neat to see the animals  from your room or from the viewing areas. There are lots of activities for kids. There are scavenger hunts, music activities, storytelling, beading, cookie decorating, and more. They also have really good food. If you eat at Boma, you can try lots of different African foods from the buffet. Animal Kingdom Lodge is a beautiful resort.

Madalyn, age 11, Nova Scotia, Canada

Yacht and Beach Club and Villas. The Yacht and Beach Club are so close to Epcot that you can walk there. There is even a special entrance you get to use. The pool is huge! It has a sand bottom and a long, twisting slide. It is the best pool I have ever been to. All kids should try Beaches and Cream. The ice cream is great!

Trevor, age 13, Valdosta, GA

Boardwalk Inn and Villas. Check out the entertainment and games on the Boardwalk in the evenings. I really like that this hotel is close to Epcot, so you can stroll around World Showcase or watch Illuminations. You can also walk to Hollywood Studios. The arcade is really cool. Make sure to eat breakfast at the Boardwalk Bakery. You can also get tiny Mickey Mouse cakes there.

Mariah, age 9, New Lenox, IL

Contemporary and Bay Lake Tower. If you like the Magic Kingdom, the Contemporary is a terrific choice because it is the

closest resort to Magic Kingdom with a walkway to the park. It has Chef Mickey's, and the monorail goes through the hotel. If you have a park view, you can see the fireworks from your own  balcony and can listen to the fireworks music on the TV, currently on Channel 20.

Shaina, age 10, Flagstaff, AZ

Polynesian. The volcano pool is a lot of fun. I liked seeing the water light show from the beach. You could also see the Magic Kingdom fireworks from the beach. Be sure to get a hidden Mickey sheet from the front desk. When you get to the clue that you have to go upstairs for, look on the floor.

Ashley, age 9, Shoreview, MN

Grand Floridian. The Grand Floridian was my favourite; I loved the posh Victorian style and the atmosphere. The pools were really great, too. I really liked the slide at the beach pool and the competitions they hold every day. Every night we got turndown service which was cool, as we found chocolates on our bed every night! My advice for other children is to read a copy of the information guide to check what activities are going on every day!

Jessica, age 13, Maidstone, UK

Wilderness Lodge and Villas. The resort has a relaxed atmosphere. There is so much to enjoy that you don't feel rushed to get to the parks. I think other kids would like staying at this resort because they have a really fun hidden Mickey hunt. There is also a geyser, and you could take a boat to Magic Kingdom instead of taking the bus. The slide at the pool is pretty fun, too!

Brian, age 10, and Lia, age 7, Branford, CT

Old Key West. It's always a relaxing vacation when we stay at Old Key West. I like to come back from the parks and play shuffleboard with my sister. The sandcastle slide at the main pool is also fun. The rooms are super big, so my entire family has enough room to spread out.

Joe, age 11, Grand Forks, ND

Saratoga Springs and Treehouse Villas. I really liked staying at Saratoga Springs. I could see the golf course from my room and I liked watching the golfers play. All of the pools at the resort were great, but my favorite was High Rock Springs. At night they blew up a big screen and you could swim and watch a

 Disney movie at the same time! We also liked taking the boat from Saratoga Springs to Downtown Disney!

Darren, age 8, Malvern, PA

Character Meals

The best place to meet your favorite characters is at character meals. You don't have to wait in line because they come to you! Many of the Disney resorts have character breakfasts and dinners. You can also eat with the characters at different restaurants in the theme parks.

WHERE TO DINE WITH YOUR FAVORITE PALS

Magic Kingdom
- Cinderella's Royal Table
- Crystal Palace

Epcot
- Garden Grill
- Akershus in Norway

Hollywood Studios
- Hollywood and Vine

Animal Kingdom
- Tusker House

THE BEST CHARACTER MEALS OUTSIDE THE PARKS

Chef Mickey's at the Contemporary. I've been to other character meals, but this is my favorite. I got to see Mickey, Minnie, Pluto and Goofy all in one place. It sure beat having to wait in line at a park to see them. They came to me! I ate very well that morning. They had the normal breakfast stuff (eggs, bacon, biscuits, donuts, muffins, yogurt, fruit, etc.), or you can go during dinner. One of my favorites was the Mickey waffles. You can only get them at Disney.

Austin, age 13, Fairbanks, AK

1900 Park Fare at the Grand Floridian. Dinner at 1900 Park Fare is called Cinderella's Happily Ever After Dinner. They have a big buffet with lots of different food. They also have a sundae bar for dessert. The best part of dinner is meeting the characters. You can meet Cinderella, Prince Charming, and the step-sisters. The step-sisters are the funniest characters I have ever met. If you have a little brother that irritates you, tell the step-sisters that he will marry one of them. It's so funny!

Madalyn, age 11, Nova Scotia, Canada

Ohana's at the Polynesian. We had the best breakfast at Ohana's! Lilo, Stitch, Pluto, and Mickey were there. Stitch was very funny and tried to take our fruit. If you want, you can dance around the restaurant with the characters. They have eggs, potatoes, and bacon, and you can eat as much as you want because they will bring out more. The juice is amazing!

Justin, age 10, Auburn, AL

Holidays and Special Events

A visit to Walt Disney World during the holidays is sure to be special. During the year, Walt Disney World hosts dozens of special events from sports to flowers to Star Wars; there is something for everyone to enjoy.

Flower and Garden Festival. The character sculptures are amazingly detailed and it was fun to look at the variety of plants

used. The sculptures are amazing. It was really neat to see all the Disney characters I love made out of beautiful plants and flowers. There are also playgrounds set up around the park just for the festival. There is a butterfly area that is fun for little kids.

Abigail, age 13, Grayson, GA

The character sculptures are called topiaries. A topiary is a plant that is trimmed into a shape.

Star Wars Weekends. If you are a Star Wars fan, this is a must for you! You get to meet lots of Star Wars characters and even get autographs of actors and actress who played in the Star Wars movies. We saw shows and parades and learned a lot more about Star Wars! It was really funny when the Storm troopers pulled people out of the crowds and pretended to arrest them.

Joe, age 13, Mattawan, MI

International Food and Wine Festival. I like the food and wine festival because I can try different foods from many different countries and it is not very expensive. That way I know what I like and can get it again later, or another day, if I want to. You get to learn about other cultures this way. They have different booths set up so there are more countries there than usual, although my favorite is there all year long—crepes in France.

Alex, age 10, Gardner, Kansas

Mickey's Not-So-Scary Halloween Party. This is a fun party where you can dress up in costume and trick-or-treat for candy. They give you a bag and you can fill it up. There are lots of characters, and they are all dressed up for Halloween, too!  There is a different parade and fireworks that are especially fun. During the parade, the headless horseman runs down Main Street. It was awesome!

Issac, age 12, Mesa, AZ

Mickey's Very Merry Christmas Party. This is a special party during the holidays. They serve complementary hot chocolate,  cookies, apple juice, and apple slices. They have a special parade and even special maps to show which rides will be open. They also have dance parties with the characters and special shows. The castle has a ton of Christmas lights on it and just looks so pretty! It also snows on Main Street! The party was so much fun!

Shelby, age 9, Beaverton, OR

Osborne Family Spectacle of Dancing Lights. If you go to Hollywood Studios during the Christmas season, you'll get a chance to see the Osborne Family Spectacle of Dancing Lights. It's a huge display of Christmas lights that every so often perform a short light show set to Christmas music. It's fun to try to find the black cat Halloween decoration mixed in with the Christmas lights.

Brooke, age 11, Shelby Township, MI

Epcot Holiday Storytellers. During Christmas at Epcot, you can see different holiday storytellers from around the world tell their story of Christmas. Canada is my favorite storyteller. Papa Noel comes out and tells you about Canada's Christmas. Also, Canada is awesome!

Alyssa, age 12, Milton, FL

Take a pirate cruise. At some of the resorts you can take a Pirate Cruise! The Cast Members make you an honorary pirate and you get to go on a cruise to find treasure. It's so neat, and the Cast Members are great at acting out the whole story. You get to go without your mom and dad. I loved yelling "Aaaarrgh!" at all the other boats we saw on the lagoon!

Katie, age 10, Indian Trail, NC

ESPN the Weekend

Other special events include ESPN the Weekend, musical concerts, and marathons.

Kid Tipster Resources

BECOME A KID TIPSTER

☑ **Do you like to travel?**

☑ **Do you love Walt Disney World?**

☑ **Are you a keen observer? (someone who pays close attention)**

If you answered **YES** to the above questions, you would make a great Kid Tipster! Visit http://vacationfieldguides.com to rate the Walt Disney World attractions and submit your own tips. You can also email your suggestions to kidtips@vacationfieldguides.com or fill out the survey on page 125 and mail it to me. I can't wait to hear from you and read your tips!

Coming soon from Vacation Field Guides:
- *Kid Tips for Disneyland*
- *Kid Tips for a Disney Cruise*
- *Walt Disney World Adventure*

Trip Planning

Planning your trip is a lot of fun! Use these pages to help you keep track of your vacation details.

Trip Details

I am going on vacation with _____

_____

We are visiting Walt Disney World in

_____ for _____days.
　　　month

We are staying at _____.
　　　　　　　　　　　name of resort

We are traveling to Walt Disney World by
- Plane
- Train
- Car
- Bus
- Boat

I am really looking forward to

The theme park I want to visit first

My top three must-see attractions

Magic Kingdom	Epcot
1.	1.
2.	2.
3.	3.
Disney's Hollywood Studios	**Disney's Animal Kingdom**
1.	1.
2.	2.
3.	3.

A snack or restaurant I want to try

The characters I want to meet
- Mickey Mouse
- Donald Duck
- Goofy
- Pluto
- Chip & Dale
- Cinderella
- Ariel
- Snow White
- Belle
- Aurora
- Buzz Lightyear
- Stitch
- Lilo
- Mary Poppins
- Alice in Wonderland
- Peter Pan
- Tinker Bell
- Winnie the Pooh
- Tigger
- Eeyore
- _____
- _____
- _____
- _____

A souvenir I would like to buy

I plan to write postcards to

Packing Suggestions

- o Sweatshirt/Sweater
- o Shorts/Pants
- o Shirts
- o Bathing Suit/Goggles
- o Sunscreen
- o Hat/Sunglasses
- o Comfortable Shoes
- o Water Shoes
- o Camera
- o I-pod and headphones
- o DS/PSP
- o Book
- o Lanyard for pins
- o Toy/stuffed animal
- o Small light
- o Autograph book/pen
- o Portable Fan
- o Rain Poncho
- o Pennies and Quarters
- o Small backpack or bag
- o Addresses of friends and family to write them a postcard

Lost Card

No one plans to get separated from his or her parents while on vacation, but parents sometimes get lost. The most important thing you can do is remain calm and find a Cast Member who can help you find your missing parents. Some families decide on a meeting spot in each park just in case they become separated.

Cut out the card below and fold it in half along the solid line. Fill out the information, cover the card with packing tape or scotch tape to protect it, and slip in into your pocket each day.

Lost Card Directions

1. Stay where you are.
2. Find a Cast Member. (They have on the special name tags.)
3. Give them this card, or tell them you need to call your parents.

My name is_____

I am staying at this hotel _____

_____

My parent's cell phone numbers are:

_____

_____

Share Your Tips

Do you agree or disagree with the tips in this book? Share your advice, and you just might be featured in the next edition of *Kid Tips for Walt Disney World.*

Complete the survey below and mail it to:

> Vacation Field Guides Kid Tips
> P.O. Box 366
> Pleasant Lake, MI 49272-0366

Or fill the survey out online at http://vacationfieldguides.com

Name:_____age:_____

City:_____State:_____

1. Circle the Walt Disney World theme park you like best.

   A. Magic Kingdom   C. Hollywood Studios

   B. Epcot   D. Animal Kingdom

2. The best snack at Walt Disney World is_____

3. My favorite restaurant at Walt Disney World is _____

_____

4. Kids should eat at this restaurant because_____

_____

_____

_____

_____

5. Three awesome rides that are worth waiting in line twice for
   are
   1._____

   2._____

   3._____

Pick one awesome ride and explain what you liked about the
ride. Include as many details as you can.

_____

_____

_____

_____

_____

_____

6. Three good rides that everyone should ride at least once are
   1._____

   2._____

   3._____

Pick one good ride from above and explain what you thought
was good about the ride. Include as many details as you can.

_____

_____

_____

_____

_____

7. Three rides that are ok, but could be skipped if the lines are really long are

1._____

2._____

3._____

Pick one ok ride from above and explain what you liked or didn't like about the ride. Include as many details as you can.

_____

_____

_____

_____

_____

8. The best Walt Disney World Resort is _____

_____

_____

_____

_____

9. My advice for kids traveling to Walt Disney World is _____

_____

_____

_____

_____

10. What I like best about this book_____

_____

11. I think this book would be better if _____

_____

12. The tip I found most helpful was _____

_____

Your signature:_____

A parent's signature:_____

Final Thoughts

Walt Disney World
is the best trip you
will ever take.
Alex, age 11,
Olathe, KS

Everything at Disney
is GREAT!!!
Dakota, age 7,
Spring Garden, AL

Walt Disney World
is fun for all ages.
Alison, age 8,
Lockport, IL

Disney is a great place
to have fun or just
relax.
Dante, age 12,
Warner Robins, GA

When I think Disney
World, I think "magic."
Maddy, age 10,
San Ramon, CA

Walt Disney World
is my favorite place
to go!
Carter, age 13,
Dallas, TX

"Every child is born blessed with a vivid imagination."

Walt Disney

9186109R0

Made in the USA
Lexington, KY
06 April 2011